Building Self-Esteem

THE CHRISTIAN DIMENSION

ANSELM GRUEN

Translated by John Cumming

A Crossroad Book
The Crossroad Publishing Company
New York

First published in the U.S.A. in 2000 by
THE CROSSROAD PUBLISHING COMPANY
370 Lexington Avenue,
New York, NY 10017

First published as *The Spirit of Self-Esteem*
in Great Britain in 2000 by
BURNS & OATES
Wellwood, North Farm Road,
Tunbridge Wells, Kent TN2 3DR

Original German edition: *Selbstwert entwickeln - Ohnmacht meistern*, Kreuz Verlag
1995. Copyright © Dieter Breitsohl AG Literarische Agentur Zurich 1994.

English translation Copyright © Burns & Oates/Search Press Limited, 2000

The Scripture quotations contained herein are from the *New Revised Standard Version
Bible*, copyright © 1989 by the Division of Christian Education of the National Council
of Churches of Christ in the USA, and are used by permission. All rights reserved. When
the emphasis of the German version used by the author requires it, recourse has been had
to the *New English Bible*, copyright © The Delegates of the Oxford University Press
and The Syndics of the Cambridge University Press 1960, 1971, and *The New Testament
in Modern English* by J. B. Philips, copyright © J. B. Philips 1960, with adaptations.

Library of Congress Cataloging-in-Publication Data
is available from the Library of Congress
ISBN 0 8245 1839 X

Typeset by Shelleys The Printers, Sherborne
Printed and bound in Great Britain by
MPG Books Ltd, Bodmin, Cornwall

Contents

How people feel about themselves   7
Self-respect, self-awareness, self-confidence;
Dispossessed, powerless, hopeless

I ACQUIRING SELF-ESTEEM   15
1. Developing self-respect   17
Basic confidence; Uniqueness; The full pot;
Accepting your shadow; The spiritual you

2. People without self-esteem   33
Small; Paralyzed; Whingeing; Running scared;
Handicapped; Conformist; Arrogant

3. Learning self-confidence   54
Self-acceptance; Self-awareness; Knowing your body;
Knowing your faith; Meditating on the Bible;
Celebrating feasts; The Pauline way; Reconciliation;
The mystical way

II REMAKING THE REAL YOU   87
1. Powerlessness   90
Feeling ineffectual; Helpless with others;
The state of the world

2. The results of powerlessness   101
Anger and aggression; Violence and brutality;
Unyielding rigour; Self-punishment;
Resignation and despair

3. Dealing with powerlessness   109
A. *Human ways*   109
With others; On your own; Useful rituals;
Freeing yourself from others' power; Dealing with power
B. *Religious ways*   119
Humans are empowered;
Freeing yourself from the world's power;
Coming to terms with your own lack of power;
Prayer and empowerment; Sharing in Christ's power;
The power of prayer; The power of love

Summary   137

Notes   141

About the author   143

How people feel about themselves

As a counsellor, I have experienced the same thing again and again: a vast number of people have problems that can be traced back to a basic lack of self-esteem and to a deep-seated conviction that they are powerless and ineffectual.

These are not only young people who, like so many others in their age-group, haven't built up enough confidence in themselves to face the world effectively, and desperately long for the self-respect needed to forge a secure personality and to weather the storms of life. Middle-aged people, too, often tell me how much they suffer from a lack of self-esteem. They are afraid to say what they think when other people talk and behave confidently. They don't trust themselves. They are convinced that others can say or do it all better than them.

Mothers are especially liable to feel like this when their children have left home. They suddenly notice that the self-confidence they had acquired over all those years of caring and nurture collapses and disappears. In fact, they had defined themselves in relation to their children. What they meant to themselves was being those children's mothers. In the past they could come up with that answer at least, if they had to ask themselves who they were. But now they have to face their real selves. They soon begin to suspect that the hard truth is they aren't anyone at all, or anyone worth mentioning.

Older people, too, often admit to having a pretty low opinion of themselves. Much later in life they remember very clearly how they never seemed to count for much

when they were children. People didn't take them seriously
or ask them what they thought about this or that. Now,
when they're too old to do anything of value, they feel
quite worthless.

Young people, of course, tend to suspect that they are
useless. They agonize about not being taken seriously,
wonder whether they are too inhibited, and are afraid they
are not as street-wise as they ought to be. They worry
about blushing as soon as someone raises a subject that
they find difficult to cope with, or that makes them
uncomfortable. Their main fear is that perhaps no one
really likes them and they are not worth knowing or lovable
in any way. Young men are inhibited with young women
because they are unsure whether they are accepted by
them. If they see other men with girl-friends, their self-
esteem drops to an all-time low. Unlike everyone else (so it
seems), they are still on their own and no girl has ever fallen
for them. Women are afraid that men won't take them
seriously, and believe that people find them sad or boring
because they don't measure up to the current ideal of
beauty. So they devote all their energy to making sure they
look exactly as they think men expect them to look.

Feeling useless, inept and powerless is something that
constantly comes up in pastoral work. One young man or
woman may suddenly find he or she just can't make a
decision about his or her future. Others experience their
lack of control over things when they are first called on to
exercise some responsibility, to organize themselves, or
merely have to fight the couch-potato syndrome: the
general inclination nowadays to vegetate and just do
nothing. They simply can't take it any farther, think it all
out, get anything done. They constantly tell themselves
that they might have failed that time, but now they will get
a grip on themselves. Then it happens again, and again, and
again. Eventually they discover the horrible truth: they just
can't change.

Young women hate themselves for not being able to tackle their eating problems. Young men feel useless when their sexual feelings and behaviour don't match up to received concepts of what sex should be, or to their idealistic notions of it. Others worry about continually finding fault with themselves, feeling guilty or hesitant and uncertain in front of others, and making mistakes but not being able to do anything about it.

External circumstances—social or political conditions we can't directly influence, perhaps—are often responsible for feelings of powerlessness, as when people are trying to find a job. Anyone who has finished school or higher education and sends off forty or fifty applications for posts without any result whatsoever will feel uncertain about the future. A suspicion dawns that whatever you do it just won't change the situation. As an individual you can't alter grim reality, so it seems.

Young people who at school or university became enthusiastic campaigners for a better environment often give up caring, and say that it all seems meaningless anyway. Whatever they do personally, most of the world couldn't care less about nature and everyone carries on wasting, spoiling and ruining things in the same old way.

Then there are those who feel powerless to save their marriage when it begins to break up, or to do anything about changing or rescuing a relationship that has soured.

Many feelings of ineffectuality have their origins in childhood experience. A child may have felt powerless to reduce the tension between parents or to stop quarrels. Some people experienced a particular kind of ineffectual rage when they were unjustly punished as children. Now, as adults, they relive the same helplessness in their relations with bosses, officials, and anyone "over" them, and in conflict situations in the family, at work, in the parish, and in the community generally.

Parents feel powerless with respect to their grown-up children when they do things quite different from whatever was planned or dreamed of for them. The parents find they just can't get through to them any longer.

Old and young people alike feel helpless about a world where so many things go rotten and wrong: a world they can't influence because it is controlled and run by others, by powerful groups and by hidden forces they can't get to grips with or even see clearly.

Self-respect, self-awareness, self-confidence

There are many terms for and associated with self-esteem and powerlessness: self-respect, self-awareness and self-confidence, for example. They are certainly related and may mean much the same thing but can also signify something slightly or very different. When I discuss people's lives and problems with them, they often tell me that they lack self-awareness or self-confidence, or that they have no self-respect, self-assurance, and so on.

Someone who is self-aware and confident knows who he or she is and his or her capabilities. If you are self-confident you can stand up and carry on without anything or anyone seriously damaging your confidence. Sometimes, however, self-assurance is a mere show. Many people pretend to be self-assured when they are anything but sure of themselves. They may appear self-confident and on top of things when they actually think very little of themselves. They hide their low self-esteem under their aware, confident and assured behaviour.

Self-respect in a good sense means knowing that you are worth something. It means being convinced of your own dignity and value, of your uniqueness as a person. It is the sign of your self, of your real being, and of your God-given image.

Self-respect in the present context includes trusting in yourself, and refers more to being confident about your own feelings and trusting in God as supporting and accepting you so that you accept yourself. Confidence in your own worth and confidence that you are valued ultimately are mutually supportive. Because I know that as a human being I have an undeniable and unassailable God-given value, I am able to accept myself as I am. I am able to go forward trusting that I am good, and to be confident that I can safely appear before the world as the person I am. This doesn't necessarily mean being far too sure of yourself, never suffering from any kind of uncertainty, or being so smugly persuaded that you count for something that you ignore people, circumstances, and your own nature. You can be self-confident because you respect yourself, and yet feel or even seem somewhat uncertain in an alien environment, for you acknowledge your uncertainty, and carry on with the assurance you have or can muster. You learn how to adapt yourself, and how to negotiate your way through novelty. Then, though unsure, you are still appropriately self-confident and aware of your value. You are still valuable as a person in spite of all your uncertainty and all your inhibitions.

Whereas people who are too sure of themselves can't acknowledge or permit any kind of personal weakness or inadequacy, self-respect accepts weakness. Self-respect doesn't mean inflating yourself to an inappropriate extent. It means straightforward awareness of your own value in spite of all inadequacies and limitations.

Dispossessed, powerless, hopeless

Powerlessness can mean the state of sheer inability to comprehend, analyze or cope with a situation that affects us in times of crisis. If the difficulties or pain are so great that we just can't carry on any longer, the body often reacts by becoming "helpless," as in a fainting spell when we actually lose consciousness. In the kind of psychological fainting spells I am thinking of, we become "unconscious" so that we don't have to tackle, or even hear or contemplate, the situation we're faced with.

Powerlessness can also mean our awareness of our own lack of power, in the sense of our inability to do some particular thing, and of our failure to seize the implications and possibilities of some occasion.

You can be powerless just to go on existing, as well as powerless to act. Then you are deprived of opportunity, of influence, and of any possibility of anything in any sense, so it seems. Everything seems to have been taken away from you. You feel dispossessed. People who are powerless like that can't get anything going and can't seem to affect things. They have no possibility of changing anything, or of moulding and shaping themselves, let alone events.

But feeling powerless in one way or another is actually part and parcel of being human. Human beings are both powerful and powerless because, after all, they are just human. They have the power to control this world and themselves, but they also undeniably lack the power ultimately to control their existence. In that absolute sense, they are powerless compared with God since they are but human.

That kind of inability to affect the ultimate nature of things is an inescapable aspect of being born a human being. But the powerlessness that affects people most of all nowadays, and that drives them to distraction or apathy, is not that basic, existential condition of having been born and being at all, but the helpless feeling you have when you are unable to cope with your life, people around you, or the world as a whole. Powerlessness in this sense is often associated with inadequate self-esteem, but isn't identical with it.

Sometimes feeling powerless and inadequate self-esteem go hand-in-hand, as when you feel helpless to do anything about your own mistakes and faults, and you just can't think how you could ever change yourself in any way. Then, it seems, you are condemned to remain the same person who always gets it wrong, everywhere and for ever.

On the other hand, many people are quite self-confident and aware of themselves, and have lots of self-esteem, yet still feel helpless about this or that, or a whole range of things. In spite of their quite healthy attitude of mind, they find they are powerless in several aspects of their lives. Perhaps they feel helpless as teachers when they can't do anything with the children in their class or school, merely because the parents are hopelessly inadequate, incompetent, washed-out, or uncooperative bullies.

Others may feel powerless as priests or ministers because the number of people coming to church just goes on dropping, even though they stretch themselves to the limit trying to preach imaginatively and make the services moving and relevant. Their helplessness grows because they get scarcely any reactions to their counselling, even though they wear themselves out doing everything they can for the most difficult cases possible. On top of all that, they feel as powerless as others in face of all the injustice in the world, the universal poverty and need, wave after wave of violence, stupid and complacent bureaucracy, and senseless wars.

Hardly anyone can suffer that kind of powerlessness easily. Some people react by falling into a fairly or very deep depression, or just become resigned to it all. Others become aggressive and strike out wildly in various ways, so that they don't have to think about their own helplessness. Yet others start looking for ways of gaining and wielding power to make up for their own inability to alter things.

In the following pages I shall try to show how we can cope with our feelings of powerlessness, even though they are an inevitable part of our human existence, without being controlled and maimed by them. As a priest and counsellor, I shall try to describe various ways of developing a healthy self-esteem and sense of our own value and possibilities.

I am concerned not so much with the purely psychological level but primarily with the spiritual dimension of the subject. After all, I am a monk whose life is based on faith. I try to know and experience faith as an aid to awareness and assurance of personal purpose and value. My life is based on forging true self-confidence because I trust in God. I hope and trust that faith will always show me a way of adjusting to my lack of power and coping with it creatively and purposively. But before I can obtain this kind of help from my faith, so that I learn to live with my experience of being so helpless, and gradually develop the right kind of self-esteem and self-confidence, I have to face up to the reality of my powerlessness and acknowledge exactly what it and my inadequate self-awareness or self-esteem really mean.

In other words, the spiritual dimension can't ignore psychological reality. In fact, you can only get to the spiritual dimension, to God, through the psychological dimension. The way to God isn't some kind of spiritual bypassing of our own psychic nature. There is no kind of spiritual short-cut that can save us the trouble of looking responsibly at our own psychology.

Christ came among human beings to give us the courage to examine, and act in and on our own real world, which means who we really are. There is no other way of reaching God.

I Acquiring Self-Esteem

I want to say something about human psychology. This will provide the essential background for a discussion of how we can develop true self-esteem, and of the reasons why we suffer from inadequate confidence in ourselves. I want to show that there are ways of helping ourselves to cultivate effective self-esteem.

Experience has taught me that this is best done by combining psychology and spirituality. It is always one and the same self that has to learn how to be appropriately confident, empowered, and assertive and also stands before God as a unique person with a basic trust in life and in God.

1. Developing self-respect

Whatever happened in our childhood, each and every one of us is faced with the task of developing an appropriate degree of self-respect. Of course, the basic circumstances in which we have to tackle this problem are different for each human being. Some people may have had a childhood that gave them every reason to trust in life and in themselves. Others, however, were made to feel small and were constantly devalued and put down as children. For them, the task is much more difficult. But it is not hopeless by any means. They, too, can reach the state of mind in which they can say "Yes" to themselves and their lives, become reconciled with their strengths and weaknesses, discover their unique selves, and thus have the confidence to live with and act meaningfully in front of other people.

Basic confidence

The experience of basic trust that an infant has with its mother and acquires from her is absolutely decisive in life. If the mother radiates trust and confidence, then the same strong assurance will develop in the child. But if the mother is unsure or lost, basically afraid that she just doesn't know how to bring up a child, and constantly shows this confusion, then the child too will lack assurance and become anxious.

In the first phase of its development a child simply adopts whatever it experiences in its relationship with its mother. A child takes on board not only what a mother does but how she does it. A child knows and feels whether a mother is happy or unhappy, her life is fulfilled or rotten, and she is assured or dithering. It knows whether she is really concerned or is only pretending, and, of course, whether she really loves or just rather likes her child, or is actually full of aggressive feelings about and toward it. All these perceptions contribute to the growth of assurance or a lack of it in children, and thus to the basis of a person's self-awareness and self-esteem later in life.

Erik Erikson coined the term "basic trust."[1] Basic trust is the feeling that you can trust your parents, but also that you can trust yourself. If you have acquired this basic trust from your parents and in your family circle, you will look at the world around you with trust and confidence. You can take risks in life, and you can enjoy trying out your abilities. Your fundamental feelings about yourself are supported by profound confidence in the trustworthiness of other human beings, in fact in the trustworthiness of existence altogether. Ultimately, this basic trust also contains a religious component. Human trustworthiness also reveals something of the loyalty of God, who is always there for us, and whom we can trust ultimately.

Erikson believes that an upbringing that stresses religion and tradition "reinforces the child's basic trust in the trustworthiness of the world."[2] Faith extends the child's basic trust from people and the world to God, the ground of all being. If a child develops an inadequate degree of basic trust, it becomes excessively self-critical. It will begin to have doubts about itself, its abilities, and the possibility of other people accepting it.

Trusting in life is an essential condition for a child's acquisition of a unique personal identity, or "ego-identity." My ego-identity is the feeling that I accept all aspects of my life and that I have integrated them into my ego, or self. It is my ability to see a thread that will guide me through the labyrinth of my life, or my conviction that there is such a thread there somewhere. It is the knowledge that I have discovered the inner unity of my own being. A strong ego-identity gives a child security and assurance about its drives or impulses and protects it from the kind of harsh conscience that so often leads to masochism and the self-torture of people who lack basic trust.

People who have discovered their ego-identity are capable of intimacy and ultimately of the capacity to be truly "generative," the impulse to be fruitful and multiply. This may be expressed in having and bringing up children, or in creative achievement of one kind or another. According to Erikson, integration is the goal of human development. When you are integrated, you are one with yourself. You are integrated with and accept your own life-history. You have integrity. You have a strong self-esteem and conviction of your own unique worth.

Erikson's findings are very important for Christians too. In religious education worthy of the name, trust in a trustworthy God is the essential basis of all talk about God. But if God is always presented as an ever-present spy, monitor, or secret policeman, a child's basic attitude will not be trust but fear. Then we feel checked, controlled, restricted, watched and judged in everything we do. But it is not enough merely to talk of a God of trust. Our own attitude and behaviour must awaken trust before we can experience God as the ultimate ground of all trust.

What Erikson says is an excellent criterion for the right way to speak not only about God but about human beings. If the main thing we require from children is to be well-behaved and to obey God's commandments and our rules, we shall bring them up as suitably trained and adapted but utterly bleak and boring creatures. People as God wants them to be are integrated and creative: they are whole people, fruitful, imaginative, and productive. People who have discovered the inner unity of their lives are lively and always brimming with new ideas. When you are with them you feel somehow that something is always going on around them that is meaningful for others too. They have a certain kind of aura. People like that are simply human beings as God intended them to be.

Uniqueness

Self-respect is not only a question of trusting yourself, the world and God, but of discovering your uniqueness.

Everyone is a unique personality. Everyone is a unique image made by God: one that only that person and no one else is and has. Thomas Aquinas says that each and every one of us is a unique expression of God in this world. The world would be poorer if every single one of us were not here to express God in his or her special way. In his autobiography, Roman Guardini tells us that in the first place God says something fundamental about each human being—pronounces a special set of words over him or her, as it were—that applies to that person and to no one else. Every human being is a word of God become flesh. And our task is to make this unique something God has said perceptible and effective in life, to make sure it is heard as the extraordinary pronouncement it is.

Self-respect means knowing your own value. It means discovering the unique image of God that I am, and the special pronouncement that God makes in me alone. That won't necessarily make me superficially sure of myself, streetwise, and able to complete a deal with an up-to-date closing technique, but it will mean that I am on the way to discovering and understanding the mystery of my own existence. I shall be able to stop comparing myself with others and trying to stress my strong points. My uniqueness is independent of all the virtues I might lay claim to. It means that I was shaped by God. The Psalmist described this experience in these words: "For it was you who formed my inward parts; you knit me together in my mother's womb. I praise you, for I am fearfully and wonderfully made" (Ps. 139:13f).

John Bradshaw has shown how important it is to be aware of our uniqueness if we are to acquire the amount of self-respect we need to function proficiently. A child develops a strong sense of its own value if its parents take its uniqueness seriously, if its feelings are acknowledged, and if they allow a child to be the person it really is in front of them. Otherwise a child will react with mistrust. It will feel inwardly wounded and take refuge within itself. The result is a child closed in on itself. If you are like that as a child you are liable to have the same disposition to hide inside yourself when you are grown up. A child's uniqueness represents its likeness to God, who revealed himself as I AM. If a child isn't noticed and taken seriously as a person with all its unique feelings and its own special value (Bradshaw says), it is wounded spiritually. This spiritual assault turns us into dependent, grown-up children suffering from feelings of guilt and shame.

If we were to look into every single history of human inadequacy (and this is true of every man and every woman who suffers in this way), we would find that at some point a wonderful, valuable, special and lovable child lost its sense of assurance that "I am who I am."[3]

Young people suffering from a lack of self-respect constantly tell me that their parents never acknowledged their uniqueness. They did not try to empathize with their children. Instead they judged them by their own standards. If these children wanted to try something out, all they heard was: "You're too young to do that. You can't do that. You're too stupid. You'll never be able to understand it." Negative messages of this kind erode all self-esteem. Children adopt their parents' opinion of them, and internalize it. They begin to feel, then become convinced, that they aren't good at anything, they're too slow, others are better at whatever it is, and so on. They lose the capacity to develop a sense of their own individuality.

Their parents' judgements and criticisms devalue these children so radically that they can feel unique only in a negative sense. They are convinced that they are thicker than anyone else, the most incompetent kids on the block, and pretty well human rubbish. If I'm not unique as the person God made me, then at least I can find some kind of compensation in being uniquely awful.

The full pot

In her book on self-respect and communication, Virginia Satir, a family therapist, offers a superb image of self-valuation.[4] It is the big iron pot that stands on her farm and, depending on the season, is filled with soap, stew, or manure. She uses it to stand for various degrees of self-respect. If I say: "My pot's full today," everyone knows that I'm bursting with energy and enthusiasm. "Leave me alone, my pot's leaking!" tells the others that I'm feeling down today.

In our retreat house, the guests who are with us for two or three months trying to discover their inner resources under therapeutic and spiritual guidance soon adopt the image of the pot. One of them will suddenly call out that his pot is full to overflowing today. Others address each other as if they were the pot and become quite enthusiastic about the possibilities. One man told another he wasn't even a pot but just a cheap bucket full of holes. Another said to a fellow-retreatant that she wasn't a pot either, but a concrete-mixer. The guests catch on to this unique way of expressing their own feelings, or how they think others feel about themselves.

Self-esteem isn't genetic. It is learned in the family. Whether children feel accepted and valued depends on the messages they receive from their parents. Children notice how their parents look at them and are adept at reading underlying expressions and feelings. They know whether their parents care for them and think they're worthwhile. Children need to live in a free atmosphere if they are to develop a proper sense of their own value. They must be in an environment where people speak frankly to each other and accept mistakes. Inadequate self-valuation is often the result of poor or confused communication in a setting where no one is certain what is going on, or what anyone really thinks or believes.

But it is never too late to acquire and reinforce self-esteem. It is always possible to substitute effective for inadequate communication, and to be able to undergo new experiences that will help to fill the empty pot. By practising new ways of communicating, of talking to one another so as to elicit a response, the guests in our retreat house entered a world of mutual aid. Everyone's pot filled up in the end. Obviously the world you live in has to practise effective communication before you can acquire a genuine conviction of your own value. It certainly isn't enough for the members of a family to be pious if they can't talk to one another. Piety alone doesn't create self-esteem. Successful communication is a prerequisite of authentic community. Without it we cannot treat each other as worthwhile, appreciate our own qualities, and feel of value before God.

Accepting your shadow

True self-respect doesn't necessarily mean appearing perfectly self-assured. Your ability to accept yourself is the decisive factor.

Some years ago I gave a course for psychologists. On arriving, one of them said that he felt utterly confused and beside himself because he found driving so nervously exhausting. I was quite taken aback. I had always imagined that psychologists and psychiatrists were especially cool and quite unflappable. But I soon realized that truly self-assured people are reconciled to their weaknesses and can accept their inadequacies. If you can openly admit your mistakes and difficulties in front of others, you have acquired genuine self-respect. You can accept yourself as you are, which means along with your inefficiency and your inconvenient traits and tendencies.

Jung says that self-acceptance includes accepting your own shadow (the converse in your unconscious of whatever you stress in your ego-consciousness, or conscious self): "The inferior and even the worthless belongs to me as my shadow and gives me substance and mass. How can I be substantial without casting a shadow? I must have a dark side too if I am to be whole; and by becoming conscious of my shadow I remember once more that I am a human being like any other."[5]

People exist between two poles: between fear and trust, reason and emotion, love and aggression, discipline and lack of control. Various psychological theories of human personality talk of a continuum, or of a dualism, or use similar terms in this respect. Some people who seem outwardly self-assured are actually only in touch with one of the two poles of their personality, or sides of their dualism. A rational type may argue with great self-assurance but is never able to display his or her feelings. As soon as the conversation is seriously and inescapably focussed on the emotional aspect of life, people of this type grow nervous, begin to panic, or just clam up. Their sense of their own value isn't balanced. They are emotionally one-sided.

If you live your conscious life in terms of only one of your two poles, you repress the other. It is put into the shade, as it were; it becomes your shadow. Once repressed, it exerts a negative effect on you. Then your repressed emotion may suddenly appear in the form of sentimentality. Or repression of the part that favours lack of discipline and anarchy may cause you to lose control altogether in a particular area of life. Or the shadow self may emerge as excessive sensitivity as soon as anyone touches on your especially weak points. Then people who are usually outwardly self-aware and self-controlled suddenly lose assurance and control. Their superficial self-assurance is shattered.

But individuals who have accepted their shadows are able to react sensibly when they find themselves in a situation calling for self-criticism, when they know they have made a mistake, or when others judge them severely. They may not enjoy it, but their reaction is balanced. They know how to respond appropriately. They are quite reconciled to their good and bad points, and they are never shocked out of their minds by what people say about them. It is difficult to upset them because they know the ground they stand on has two aspects which they have come to terms with.

Jung believes that you have passed through a major stage on the way to healthy self-understanding and self-respect when you have accepted your shadow, integrated your *anima* and *animus* (the femininity and masculinity components of your soul-image), and recognize the image of God expressed in the human soul in metaphorical and symbolic forms.

Jung talks of you becoming your "self" and not of strengthening your "ego" or "I." The self is different from the ego. The ego is merely conscious. It is the conscious core of the person I am, on the basis of which I make my decisions. This is apparent, for instance, if I say: "*I* want it *now!*" Or: "Well, *that's* what *I've* decided to do!" Or: "*I* am going there." Or: "No, *I don't* want to!" The ego is the part of you that wants to take charge and run things.

We are far too often inclined to cling to the ego in us. To reach the self, I have to leave my little ego behind, as it were. I have to enter the depths of the me who I am, in order to discover the truly profound core of the person I am: my self.

Frequently, however, people do not find it easy to descend from the high point of the ego and remain at a "lower" level. But: "Unlike other religions Christianity holds up before us a symbol whose content is the individual way of life of a [human being], the Son of Man, and . . . regards this individuation process as the incarnation and revelation of God himself. Hence the development of [a person] into a self acquires a significance whose full implications have hardly begun to be appreciated, because too much attention to externals blocks the way to immediate inner experience. Were not the autonomy of the individual the secret longing of many people it would scarcely be able to survive the collective suppression either morally or spiritually."[6] Only those who acknowledge the divine images within them can discover their selves, and thus find themselves. And only those who have discovered this inner core, the true self, have a genuine sense of their own worth.

Those in contact with their selves do not have to rely on the opinions of others. They are content with themselves and acknowledge their own value. They develop the ability to act confidently on their own initiative. The journey into ourselves is so fascinating and extraordinary that praise and blame from others become unimportant when we are well on our way to self-discovery. In one of his letters Jung says: "Ultimately, an individual's worth is expressed not in his or her relationship with another person, but in his or her self. Therefore we should never allow the idea we have of ourselves, or our self-respect, to depend on the way someone else reacts to us, however human and sympathetic the involvement may be."[7] Learning to be yourself means coming to be your true self, and thus reaching a state of autonomy where you are independent of human judgements.

Jung also believes that self-valuation includes reconciliation with your own life-history. In the end it is pointless to keep delving into your past merely to look for the reasons for your own lack of self-confidence. At some point you have to take the responsibility for your own life. You have to accept your past as the material you have been given for the task before you now, which is shaping your own life. You may cut a beautiful statuette from a piece of wood, carve a breathtaking image from a stone block, or mould a lovely form from a lump of clay. But you have to treat the wood as wood, and the stone as stone, and the clay as clay. Otherwise you cannot possibly make the beautiful thing you have in mind. Our past is the material that happens to be available to us. We can make a fine shape from our past, irrespective of the material—whether it is a past of wood or stone or clay. But first we have to accept the material. We have to be reconciled to our life-history. Then it can become meaningful, and truly valuable, for us. I constantly tell the people I am counselling: "Your life-history is your capital. If you are reconciled with your own life then even its most difficult stretches will prove beneficial not only for you but for many others."

If I take the responsibility for my own life, I shall stop trying to blame other people for my own bad luck and suffering. Responsibility will open my eyes to the opportunities available only to me, and to the unique image that God has produced in me alone. But I also have to say goodbye to the far too elevated ideals that I may have identified myself with. It is not a question of becoming perfect and faultless but of becoming a whole person who is one with himself or herself, which means together with all the contradictions he or she contains.

For Jung, a healthy conception of my own value means that I appreciate my light and dark aspects: the high and low points, the good and bad, the divine and the all too human. Self-respect includes a feeling that God wants to be born in me in a unique way. Ultimately, my self is God's image in me: the unique image that God has made of me alone.

The spiritual you

Jung says that the self is more than the mere product of our life-history. The school of transpersonal psychology, which follows the insights of Jung, says that we can only discover who we really are if we examine and discard the various false identities, or identifications, that we have assembled in ourselves and piled up around us.

We often identify ourselves with our parents' opinions, and define ourselves in terms of success and achievement, recognition and confirmation, endowments and relationships. As long as we identify ourselves with our feelings and needs, with our sickness or health, we remain dependent on all that, and blind to the true reality of our authentic selves. We have to surrender the ways in which we usually identify with people, with roles, and with work and achievement, in order to discover who we really are. We have to shed our conventional identities and stereotypes in order to find our spiritual selves.

Transpersonal psychology has developed the practice of "disidentification." This means that I observe my thoughts, feelings, and emotions and then say to myself: "I can see my anger or annoyance. I observe it. But I am not identical with my anger. I am not my irritation. There is something in me that can observe my anger and is no longer controlled or affected by anger. This is my secret witness: my true self." Roberto Assagioli, an Italian psychiatrist, devised this method of disidentification. First of all you have to see and know your body, and realize that it is changeable. Then you return from your body to your spiritual self, to that centre of pure awareness which observes your changeable body but itself remains constant and unchanging. That is our true identity. Assagioli calls this spiritual self "a centre of pure self-consciousness and self-realization."[8]

Of course, we are more than the mere "I," or ego, that wants to make itself felt and dominate, and appears so certain and self-assured. The spiritual self is the inner country where we are wholly at home, and where we discover that our true self has been shaped by God. The spiritual self is the unique and irreplaceable image that God has made of each of us. Therefore it is not a matter of merely trying to appear self-assured and self-confident. We are more than what we appear to be in the external circumstances of our lives, whether we are assured or ill-at-ease in them, and whether our behaviour makes us seem strong or weak. Accordingly, we have to free ourselves from our estimate of ourselves. We have to look at ourselves very differently.

It is not important how I assess myself: whether I think I am better and stronger than other people. I won't discover my authentic self merely by examining the psychic wounds of my childhood and by analyzing the fears and anxieties that result from my deficient self-confidence. What is decisive, however, is that I discover the mystery of my own true self.

Bugental, another transpersonal psychologist, says that our problem is that we are always looking for our selves outside: in confirmation by others, in instances of outward success, and in external security. But the self is to be found only within, in the inner world of our soul, in our true homeland. Bugental says that the country where we really belong lies within us, and there we are the undisputed rulers. If we do not rediscover this age-old truth, each in his or her own way, we are condemned to wander hither and thither, seeking consolation where it can never actually be found—in the outside world.[9]

It is not sufficient to develop a strong outward self-awareness, to have an impressive appearance, to look imposing, to resist criticism, and to put up with objections and rejection. Of course that will give us the satisfying conviction that we look outwardly self-assured and self-confident. But if we haven't discovered our own true selves, the self-awareness we are so proud of might as well be built on sand. It has no real foundations because we are not in touch with our authentic selves.

My authentic self is more than the sum of all that has happened to me, of my life-history. It is more than the sum of my upbringing, education, and all the work I have done to develop myself and to make myself what I think I am now. My true self is a mystery because it is God expressing himself in a unique way. It is the original image that God shaped of me. It is the unique word of God that is intended, longs, and strives to become flesh in me. It is the primal word of God, which, as Romano Guardini says, has only one unique meaning: this singular, unrepeatable person that I am. My self is the word that is intended to come into this world through me and in me, and to be born as my true self. My spiritual self is this unique and inimitable word of God that longs and throbs in its longing to be made visible and audible in me alone.

There are many different metaphors for, and systems of, true self-valuation, invented by psychologists of different schools. But the Bible also supplies us with a wealth of images for an authentic conception of our own value. There is the image of the tree that grows from a tiny grain of mustard seed (Matt. 13:31ff). A man took a tiny grain of mustard seed and sowed it in his field. It was the smallest of all seeds but has grown to be the biggest of all plants. It is now a tree so big that birds come and nest in its branches. It is so huge that its roots lie deep in the earth. The tree stands for a person who is so truly self-confident that he or she cannot be easily swayed. Such a person is deeply rooted in God. Other people can lean on him or her and find protection and comfort in his or her shade.

Then there is the image of the treasure buried in a field (Matt. 13:44ff). This inestimably valuable treasure stands for my own self. There it is, buried in the field, in common earth and muck. To find my real self I have to dig into the earth.

There is also the image of the single pearl of great value (Matt. 13:45ff). The pearl grows in a wound in the flesh of an oyster. Just so, I can find my self, the image that God has made of me, in among all my wounds, pains, and traumas. In fact, this particular wound cracks open all the false images that I have erected of myself and that have covered up my own true self: the single pearl of inestimable value.

The Bible uses these illustrations to show us who we really are, and that the self is a mystery in which God himself appears and through which we can share in God. The Bible wants to show us that we are more than our life-history and the past that has formed us. This is also obvious in the story of the old tree stump from which a new sprig suddenly appears. A new shoot of life grows from what has been hacked down, torn, cut about and is, so it seems, ruined for ever. The self is not something that we can grasp and hold on to, just like that. It only becomes visible when we hack down and clear away something in our lives. The comforting message of the Bible is that this self can always reappear among the ruins of our life. It can always blossom and console other people at the very spot where everything seemed unfruitful or even dead (cf. Isa. 11:1). This is a comforting image, for it does not confuse my self with outward success and security, but discloses a self formed by God, yet revealed in the midst of my failures, injuries, and psychic bruises. It is a self that can survive all external wounds and destruction because it comes from the hand of God.

2. People without self-esteem

More and more people with insufficient self-esteem come to me to ask for pastoral advice and care. They often explain their problems by saying that they have no self-confidence, and don't think much of themselves. I sometimes have the impression that people are relieved to be able to cite a lack of self-esteem as the supposed cause of their difficulties. Nevertheless, the essential question is how they can improve their opinion of themselves, and what they should do to be more confident. In the following sections I shall offer a number of illustrations of inadequate self-confidence, as examples often say more than psychological theories and models. Here again, I shall keep to instances from the Bible, and try to show how they relate to our theme.

Small

When people discuss colleagues at work, or friends, you often hear them say that someone is difficult or peculiar because he or she has an "inferiority complex" (or even "complexes"). Every amateur psychologist knows this key-term of Alfred Adler's "individual psychology."[10]

Some people compensate for an inferiority complex by trying to be particularly charming or appealing. Others hide it behind arrogant behaviour. They construct a self-assured front, and hold their heads above the ordinary mob so that they can look down on other people. This is often a sign that the fancy façade conceals no solid, respectable building but only a miserable little hut. This is precisely what a conceited person is trying to hide behind his or her unbearable assurance. Others compensate for their inferiority by spending too much or by over-emphasizing their abilities.

The story of Zacchaeus offers a typical example of an inferiority complex and an attempt to compensate for it (Luke 19:1-10). We are told that Zacchaeus, a chief collector of taxes, was very short. Of course the author is referring to people who feel small and therefore have to make themselves big in some way. Zacchaeus tries to make up for his feelings of inferiority by earning as much money as he can. Since he is the head tax man, he concentrates on amassing wealth ruthlessly. If he is the richest man around, he thinks, then everyone will notice and respect him. But the opposite happens. The more he tries to compensate for his inferiority by grabbing as much as he can, the more inclined people are to reject him. Religious people treat him as a sinner and won't have anything to do with him. He is in the typical no-win situation of many "small" people who try to compensate for their inferiority by being attractive, by being the best in the class, or by heaping up cash. They desperately want to make an impression on other people and are always describing all the things they can do and the wonderful experiences they have had. But the more they stress their importance and their exceptional this or that, the more people tend to despise them. That is our usual reaction when someone in our street or parish, in our firm, or in the family, is always boasting. They are always objectionable. The saying "Braggarts are always happy" isn't literally true. It carries the unspoken ironic addition: "Because they're always pleased with themselves." In other words, they're oblivious to the effects of their bragging. People who show off to compensate for their inferiority are always shunned in one way or another, and enjoy life less than they appear to.

Jesus cures Zacchaeus' low self-esteem simply by looking at him and inviting himself to a meal at his house. He doesn't judge or reproach him, but accepts him without any reservation. The experience of being accepted unconditionally transforms the rich and miserly tax collector. As a result he does more than his pious critics. He gives half his property to the poor, and if he has swindled anyone out of anything, promises to pay him or her back four times as much. He no longer has to look big. Now he can live normally with people and share his possessions and life with them. He feels like a normal person, a member of the community. Then all the tax collectors and sinners come to his house and share a meal with Jesus, who shows them God's mercy and humanity.

Alfred Adler says that you can cure an inferiority complex only by common humanity, by a sense of community. This is precisely what the author of the story of Zacchaeus in the Gospel according to Luke was trying to convey. It is not self-centredness, or seeking for recognition and acceptance, that produces greater self-respect, but readiness to trust yourself with other people, and to share your life with them. You experience your own worth by sharing your life with others, and by living as an accepted member of the human community.

Paralyzed

Jesus heals a paralyzed man whose bed four people let down through an opening in the roof, so that he can lie at Jesus' feet (Mark 2:1-12). Jesus sees that the man's paralysis is something more than a outward, physical problem. It is the external expression of an internal disposition, or attitude. So the first thing Jesus does is to tell the man that his sins are forgiven.

The paralytic has to change his inner attitude to life before his infirmity can be cured and he can stand up again.

People suffering from a lack of self-esteem often feel paralyzed. They are blocked in the presence of certain other persons. They feel totally hemmed in by their limitations and imprisoned in their own confines. They dare not say what they think. They allow others so much power that they become over-inhibited in the presence of people they think are superior. Or they just can't trust themselves to say anything in a group. They are always afraid that they will express themselves pathetically and that the others might grin or even laugh at what they say.

The paralyzed man in the story is not self-possessed. He is always watching other people, trying to imagine what they might be thinking and what kind of impression he is making on them. People of this type often believe that others are thinking about them, laughing at them, and constantly criticizing them. They refer everything they see in other people to themselves. This tends to paralyze them.

A woman may enter a church and think everyone there is looking at her. Throughout the entire service, in fact, she is desperate to leave and escape this overwhelming crowd of censorious watchers. You might say she goes to church to be tortured by wanting to leave as soon as possible. In reality, of course, no one has even noticed her.

People without any self-respect very often think that others are permanently scrutinizing them and talking about them.

A man may be on a railway train and imagine that the young people opposite who are so convulsed with laughter are making fun of him. In fact they are still amused by something that happened to the group before they got on the train.

People who aren't secure in themselves refer everything to themselves. Their minds are constantly at work on these lines: "They're talking about me. They're watching me. They can see how nervous I am. They're summing me up. They're persecuting me." Inevitably, it goes from bad to worse.

I experienced this myself after ordination, when I had just taken my final degree in theology. I started a course in management science. Yes, I was a priest and I had a degree and all that, but in fact I was quite unsure of my role generally and specifically. And things weren't going well in my personal life. I found travelling to the university by tram (street car) every day a terrible ordeal. I was convinced that everyone was staring at me. I had lost all self-assurance. All I could do was hide. I got my head down in a book or my lecture notes, and tried to cut off from everyone around me. It was no use. And it didn't help when I tried reasoning with myself, saying: "Look, be rational. You're intelligent. You know they just aren't watching you." I had to go further, change the emphasis, and keep telling myself: "Well, all right, perhaps they are watching you—but so what? That's their problem, not yours. They're them. You're you. You don't give a damn. Keep reminding yourself: I'm me, not them." It was hard going, but this insistence on my individuality rather than on reason gradually helped me to become more independent of other people.

One woman who came to see me a while ago revealed her profound lack of self-respect as soon as she said she felt she was always under her husband's control. I asked her to consider for a moment whether her husband was really trying to run her life, or what she meant was that she wondered if he was (which was the same as saying she might be imagining the whole thing). She eventually admitted that any question her husband asked her amounted to a form of control or criticism as far as she was concerned. More than that (it turned out), because she had no self-respect, she was now at the stage of treating whatever her husband said as a form of rejection. Consequently, whenever her husband said anything at all, she automatically felt rejected. He might as well have slapped her in the face. So: "My husband opens his mouth" = "I'm no one." The repeated experience was very real: she felt utterly paralyzed. She was sure (she said) that her husband didn't take her seriously, but the truth was that she didn't take herself seriously. She was quite without self-confidence and self-reliance. Of course, it wasn't just her husband, as I discovered. She was absolutely convinced that people in general didn't take her seriously. In reality other people liked her quite a lot. But she didn't value herself, and therefore felt no one else could possibly think she was worthwhile. Because she didn't take herself seriously, she was sure no one else did.

If both husband and wife suffer from low self-esteem, they usually find it impossible to argue objectively. Each of them interprets his or her partner's remarks as a personal attack, and immediately reacts defensively and has to justify himself or herself. The least criticism takes the ground from under such people's feet, and they have to assert themselves emotively. They are afraid of losing and feel compelled to sting or wound each other to be one up in a lifelong contest. The result is pointless and unedifying, an ongoing row, a kind of permanent domestic trench-warfare.

All Jesus does to heal the paralyzed man is tell him to: "Get up, pick up your bed and go home!" (Mark 2:11). He says this to stop the paralytic eternally focussing on himself and worrying over and over again whether he might ever be able to walk properly and actually stand up on his own. All this thinking about it prevents him from simply getting up.

When I gave a course on the psychoanalytic interpretation of the scriptures for psychologists and psychiatrists, they were fascinated by Jesus' confrontational approach to therapy. One of them said it was generally accepted that the main aim of psychology was to understand the person in question, but that he had realized that understanding wasn't enough. He could see why Jesus resorted to confrontation.

Jesus uses the method to remove the sick man's illusions. He leaves him no way out. He has to face the truth about himself at last. No excuses are possible now. There's nothing left but to get up and walk. He has to spring to his feet, pick up the bed (the symbol of his illness), tuck it under his arm, and walk off in full view of everyone.

We would all like to shed our inhibitions and uncertainty. Our inadequacies and psychic injuries constantly upset and annoy us, to say the least. We are always worrying about them, and long to be able to stand up and walk away from them. Yet we think that we shall be able to do that only when we are sure that other people no longer notice our weaknesses and anxieties. But Jesus tells us to take hold of our inhibitions; to tuck them under our arm, so to speak; and to treat them lightly, instead of letting them maim and paralyze us. The bed we carry reminds us and others that we are still uncertain and inhibited. But that does not mean that we are tied to our bed of troubles, and can't get up from it. We're not on the ground any longer. Instead we cope with our bed by picking it up and carrying it around with us, without letting it rule our lives.

Whingeing

In the fifth chapter of the Gospel according to John, the sick man who has been like that for thirty-eight years thinks that he is ill because he is too slow, or hasn't the same opportunities and help as the others at the pool, and can't get into the water to be healed like them: "You see, I just haven't got anybody to put me into the pool when the water is all stirred up. While I'm trying to get there somebody else gets down into it first."

Making comparisons is often an expression of inadequate self-esteem. People who are always comparing themselves with others aren't in touch with themselves. They can't assess their own value or their own lives. They define themselves only by comparison with others. Then they always seem worse off than others. There are always people who are quicker on the uptake, more talented, more popular, better-looking than me. As long as I compare myself with others I don't feel right in my own skin. I don't really know who I am.

A woman may be pleased when she is asked to join a women's group. But she often feels out of place at the meetings. She keeps comparing herself with the others. They went to college or university; she didn't. The others can talk more fluently or convincingly than she can. What will they think if she tries to make a point in her usual clumsy way? During the discussion she is inwardly obsessed with the same thoughts. She keeps telling herself the others can do this or that better, or she mentally lists her disadvantages compared with them.

Jesus heals the dissatisfied man by telling him not to make comparisons. He looks at him lying on his back. Of course he realizes that he has been there like that for a long time. Everyone knows the situation. But Jesus actually notices him and shows him respect. He says: "Do you want to get well again?" (John 5:6). He confronts the man with himself, with his own will. Jesus implies that instead of comparing himself with the others, he should ask himself what he really wants to do with his life.

Jesus cuts short the dreary old dissatisfied ramble. It doesn't matter what the others do and say, how talented they are, whether they're better at something, or get things done more rapidly. All that matters is what I myself do with my life, and whether I am responsible for myself. When the sick man starts comparing himself with the others in order to evade Jesus' question, Jesus tells him (much as he did the man in the last story): "Get up! Pick up your bed and walk!" (John 5:8). You can get up. You can walk. Stop comparing. Stop complaining. Stop whining! Get up, take hold of yourself, face the world, stand upright! You can walk. Jesus meets him later in the Temple and says: "Look: you are a fit man now!"

Running scared

The story known as the parable of the talents is also about comparisons. This is the tale of the man going abroad who calls his household servants together before he goes and hands his money over to them to manage. He gives one fifty thousand pounds, another twenty thousand, and another ten thousand, according to their abilities. The third servant thinks he's hard done by compared with the others. He digs a hole in the ground and hides his master's money.

Another aspect of inadequate self-esteem—fear—is the point here. When the master comes back and goes through the accounts, the third servant makes excuses: "Sir, I always knew you were a hard man, reaping where you never sowed and collecting where you never laid out. So I was scared and I went off and hid your ten thousand pounds in the ground. Here is your money, intact" (Matt. 25:24ff). Because he is afraid of his master he hides the money to make sure things will go on as before. He is afraid that he might get things wrong and the accounts won't come out right. He is afraid he might lose by speculating. Fear makes him take precautions. He wants to avoid making a mistake at all costs. He only wants to bet on a certainty. So fear forces him to control himself and his life. He buries the money in order to keep control of it. But it is a basic rule of life that those who try to make sure of absolutely everything will lose control of their lives at one point or another. A life ruled by fear always ends up in howling and gnashing of teeth. The real truth is: the third servant is afraid of God.

Many people lack self-esteem because they have been taught about a God who strikes terror into people. Our self-image is heavily dependent on our image of God. The way we see God is the strongest archetype, or fundamental image, in us. It has the greatest effect on the way in which we experience ourselves and see ourselves. If the picture you have of God when you are a child is terrifying, and whenever you think of God you are afraid, then you are likely to become someone who buries things and tries to control everything. Your self-image is disastrous. You are not only afraid of God but of everything that might threaten you. Of anything and everything, in other words. You are afraid of death, afraid of failure, afraid of making a mistake in front of other people.

With the parable of the talents, Jesus wants to show that people like that, with a frightening image of God, haven't a chance. They always lose out. They even lose what they have basically: "As for the man who has nothing, even his 'nothing' will be taken away from him" (Matt. 25:29). By describing the consequences of fear, Jesus is asking us to follow the way of trust; to take a chance with our lives; to risk our lives. It is not a question of increasing our investments, but of taking the risk of living effectively.

If children experience God as an accountant or as an arbitrary ruler, or see him as a strict and punitive judge, they will never develop a sense of their own value. If I am always monitored by an accountant-god who records everything I do, I have no opportunity to experience myself as someone of value. I feel constantly supervised and judged.

When they were children, many men and women were told about a God who begrudges them any joy in life, who oppresses and humiliates them, and who judges them instead of supporting them. A cruel image of God always results in an inadequate or destructive self-image. The image of a punitive God is often internalized and recalled in a harsh conscience that leads people to torment, punish, constantly undervalue and devalue themselves.

An interiorized horror-image of God exerts its destructive power in a cruel conscience and allows no room for self-defence. Fear of God leads to fear of yourself, and of the depths of your own soul. You can't trust yourself to look into yourself and accept everything inside yourself.

Obviously men and women experience these psychic wounds caused by inappropriate images of God in different ways.

Male self-esteem is grossly impaired by a God who rewards only the meek: a God before whom they have to beg for everything and remain passive and receptive but never become co-operative and creative. Men can never enjoy anything approaching true self-respect if their God always makes them feel they are not just sinners but, even worse, wimps.

Many women have been psychically degraded by a one-sided male image of God, and by a purely rational theology that implicitly devalues not only the emotions but being a woman. In Catholic circles women often feel devalued by their exclusion from the priesthood. In certain hard-line Protestant and other fundamentalist churches and, of course, some Catholic groups, women feel compelled to deny their female sexuality and act as if they were asexual or neuter. In religious settings of that kind it is difficult for women to feel valued and develop anything approaching authentic self-esteem.

Handicapped

Probably the most appalling devaluation of human piety is that associated with a false idea of humility. For some people humility means self-abasement, self-devaluation and self-destruction. We are not allowed to take pride in our positive God-given qualities. We are even invited to reject justifiable pride in ourselves as arrogance toward God.

When Jesus says: "Everyone who makes himself important will become insignificant, while the man who makes himself significant will find himself unimportant" (Luke 14:11), he means: whoever has the courage to descend into his or her own reality, into the darkness of his or her own soul, will have the power to ascend to God. People who have the courage to accept their mortality or earthiness (the Latin word *humilitas* = humility, from *humus* = earth) understand who God is and are closer to God. In that sense humility is a very recent attitude in the Christian Church. It means the courage to follow the road that leads down into our very own reality, into the shadow of our own self; and to take it because it is the best way to reach God.

In the past, however, we have often misunderstood humility as a kind of disability that's somehow "good for you." Christians have misinterpreted it as a self-imposed psychological handicap by which we choose to make ourselves small, devalue ourselves, refuse to believe that we are capable of anything ourselves, and continually make excuses to ourselves for being who we are—in fact, for existing at all.

The total misunderstanding of humility so often put forward in the churches in the past is a complete falsification of what Jesus really wanted to say. It has led many Christians to humiliate themselves and to devalue everything good and powerful in themselves as unacceptable pride. All that this notion of humility has produced is a denial of the divine glory that can and should shine out in every human being.

A false idea of humility has twisted and maimed people psychologically. Of course Jesus does not want people to injure themselves and become psychic cripples. He wants them to be as upright and whole as they are intended to be. The author of the Gospel according to Luke makes this clear in the well-known story of the woman who had been bent double for many years (Luke 13:10-17): "In the congregation was a woman who for eighteen years had been ill from some psychological cause; she was bent double and was quite unable to straighten herself up." The woman's bent back reveals her low self-esteem. She just cannot face life. She cannot assert her own dignity. She is bent double by the burden of being alive. Perhaps other people oppressed and repressed her, to such an extent that she gave up trying to be herself. Someone possibly broke her spine in the sense that one day she just couldn't take the humiliation any longer. Perhaps she banished all her repressed emotions to her back. Perhaps she put them out of sight behind her, as it were, where they nevertheless weigh her down to nullity. But in the end, even in that way, she finds she can't carry the burden of the emotions she refused to acknowledge.

Jesus straightens the woman up by looking directly at her, reminding her that she exists and who she is, and facing her in one uncompromising confrontation with all the positive things he can see in her. This sudden tenderness shocks her out of herself. He doesn't simply say: "Keep your head up!" but touches her to show his concern, so that she herself begins to get in touch with the power and value of her own personality: "When Jesus noticed her, he called out and said: 'You are set free from your illness!' And he put his hands upon her, and at once she stood upright and praised God." When she feels the reality of Jesus' love, she can stand up immediately. Now she is aware of her incontestable value and dignity as a woman and, even though she is in the middle of the synagogue, she is not afraid to start praising God out loud.

Jesus wants people to stand up, be themselves, and assert the truth, whereas the president of the synagogue, who is just as spineless as the woman was (but for different reasons), hides his humanity behind rigid obedience to the religious rules, and subjection to the letter of the law: "He announced to the congregation: 'There are six days on which men may work. Come on one of them and be healed and not on the Sabbath day!' But the Lord answered him saying: 'You hypocrites . . . !'"

Jesus helps the woman to stand up and be herself on the Sabbath day, in the midst of the congregation, and while a religious service is in progress. Clearly, he wants to show us the real meaning of worship. We certainly do not worship God or perform any kind of divine service if we put burdens on people, give them a guilty conscience, and ask them to bow down before God as sinners and make themselves small and insignificant.

Jesus believes that the only kind of church service worth having is one in which people stand up as authentic individuals and realize their indisputable dignity and value, which, after all, God himself has given them. The God who has given us his own divine dignity and worth certainly has a message for us: it is that we should stand up straight and respect all that is good and positive in ourselves.

When I give courses, at the beginning of a session I sometimes ask everyone (myself included) to stand up and stay like that for a while, so that we can actually sense the link between heaven and earth. Next we let our heads drop right down, and then our shoulders. As soon as we do that we feel restricted, and begin to cut off the flow of fresh air into our bodies. Then we all walk around the room in that cramped-up or listless, unassertive posture until it takes hold of us. All we can see of the world is the limited area around our feet. Our image and understanding of the world grow darker. We begin to feel depressed. Then I start straightening people up, one by one, by touching their backs. When I have gently massaged someone's spine with my hands for a while, he or she straightens up of his or her own accord. Symbolically, but also actually, my touch has not humiliated that person but put him or her in contact once again with the individual power that, even in that short space of time, had drained away into darkness, tedium and resignation.

For me, the healing of the woman bent double is an image of our Christian life. We show that we are disciples of Christ if we realize our indisputable human value. We show our belief in Christ's resurrection if we walk upright through the world. We are more than our everyday life with all its worries and concerns. We are sons and daughters of God. In church services we rehearse our dignity as children of God when we process with our heads erect or praise God with outstretched arms. We lay claim to our self-respect not by our achievements but by reason of the dignity God has given us. Jesus did not see us primarily as sinners but essentially as sons and daughters of God sharing in the life of God.

Therefore constant insistence on sin is totally contrary to the spirit of Jesus. There is a strong tendency in the Church to represent people as sinful from the start, and to induce a state of revulsion at their wicked selves, so that they can be urged to take refuge in God's mercy. People who see things like that are suspicious of authentic self-respect. They try to break down and negate others' self-esteem so that they have to thank God abjectly for forgiving their sins.

In one sense, admittedly, we are all sinners before God. But the message Jesus has for us is the Good News! It is the news that we are accepted by God, that we have every right to be who we are, and that God accepts us as who we are without any reservation whatsoever. He wants us to walk around with our heads held high.

In fact, the Catholic Church celebrates the straightening of the woman bent double with a special feast day. It is called the feast of the Immaculate Conception. It is a symbolic celebration of our own redemption. Properly understood, this feast tells us that there is a space inside everyone of us that sin can't get at. Every one of us is immaculate within. In that space, where Christ dwells within us, we are spared from all sin. There is no possible way in which that essential us could be sinful. There we are in touch with our true self, which is stainless, free from sin, immaculate, and so forth.

The feast celebrates what Paul's letter to the Christians at Ephesus tells us is true of each one of us. The God and Father of Our Lord Jesus Christ chose us before the foundation of the world, "to become, in Christ, his holy and blameless children living in his constant care. He planned, in his purpose of love, that we should be adopted as his own children through Jesus Christ—that we might learn to praise that glorious generosity of his which has made us welcome in the everlasting love he bears towards the Beloved . . . we are freely forgiven through that full and generous grace which has overflowed into our lives and opened our lives to the truth . . . everything that exists in heaven or earth shall find its perfection and fulfilment in him" (Eph. 1:4-6).

Jesus' primary concern is to tell us not that we are sinners but that we are sons and daughters of God, and that God has chosen us for that purpose. He wants to dwell within us, and wants us to be filled with all the riches of his grace, love and tenderness (cf. John 14:23 and Eph. 1:7ff).

The early Christians constantly thanked God for enabling them to stand up again by bringing his Son back from the dead, and by giving them an assurance of their divine dignity and value. It is not a crumpled, bent and humiliated but an upright Christian who understands the implications of what Jesus Christ offers us by becoming human, dying and rising again.

Conformist

The healing of the man with a shrivelled hand is another image of inadequate self-esteem. He stands for people who have conformed and have lost all sense of daring.

We touch one another tenderly with our hands. We use our hands to set about something, to shape things, and to be creative. The man in the New Testament story (Mark 3:1-6) has a shrivelled hand. He no longer takes any risks. Very often people with little self-esteem don't trust themselves to voice their own opinion. They would rather conform, suit themselves to circumstances, than say what they think. If they're in a discussion group they look around first and listen to the others to find out what the prevailing view is. Then they come out with the same opinion. They dare not say No if they are asked for something. They always want to be liked. But, because they want to be the right person for everyone, they remain colourless. Ultimately, they never find anyone who really wants to be their friend. Because they are so careful to do the right thing they lose the right to real life.

The reason for this conformist behaviour is that I draw my self-valuation solely from the confirmation and attention of others. I have to buy my acceptance by others. As a child I never knew what it meant to be accepted for my own sake. I was accepted only on condition that I was a good child and did what was expected of me. So I tried to adapt myself and to make myself liked by everyone. I do exactly the same thing now.

Frielingsdorf tells us that someone who has never experienced unconditional acceptance will develop strategies for survival in order to win acceptance by achievement or by adaptation. But this will not be living, but merely survival.[11] People like that are always in a state of tension about being accepted by others. Because they do not accept themselves, they are always seeking acceptance by others in order to justify their existence. They are always afraid of being rejected. They relate everything they see to themselves. They think other people are talking about them and laughing at them. Because they don't accept themselves, they believe no one else will accept them. Yet deep down they long to be truly respected by others as someone of value.

Always seeking for confirmation is actually living at a lower level. Then you are always oriented to others. You are always afraid to speak your own mind because someone might make fun of what you say.

Jesus heals the conformist by telling him to: "Stand up and come out here in front!" (Mark 3:3). Now he can't conform any longer. He has to stand up for himself. Everyone starts scrutinizing him. The Pharisees are watching closely to see if Jesus heals him on the Sabbath and thus offends against the law. Jesus does not conform. He does what he thinks is right. He stands up for his opinion and his belief that human beings are more important to God than keeping commandments. Then Jesus, "deeply hurt as he sensed their inhumanity, looked round in anger at the faces surrounding him." He looks at each of the Pharisees, who have no self-esteem but hide behind the general norm, and uses his anger to defend himself from their hardness of heart. He distances himself from them and does what he ought to do. At the same time, however, disappointed at their rigidity, he understands them, and is immensely sad to see them leading such empty lives. Yet he knows what he has to do. And he does it even though they all turn against him. He doesn't need to make people like him. He does what he senses God wants him to do, and thus behaves in a truly human way.

Arrogant

Inadequate self-respect is often concealed behind a façade of arrogance and superiority. You feel that you are better than other people. You devalue them in order to increase your own worth. You think that you are self-assured and self-aware. But it's all show. You are blind to the real you. You can't see your blind spots but think you are faultless and perfect. You are conceited.

Conceited people often make a big display of their abilities and achievements. They are out to make an impression. In fact, quite a few people are impressed by them. But perceptive people find it very off-putting when someone has to show how superior he or she is. The Bible calls people like that "blind," and often uses examples and anecdotes about the blind to bring this point out. The blind (in biblical parables, that is) refuse to see themselves and reality as they are because they find them unpleasant, and because to see things as they are would be beneath their dignity. Therefore they close their eyes to their own reality in order to carry on clinging to the illusion of their superiority.

Jesus heals the man who has been born blind, who has closed his eyes to his reality from the moment of his birth. He does so by spitting on the ground, making a sort of clay with the saliva and applying it to the man's eyes (John 9:6).

Jesus does this to confront him with the earth, the *humus*, or soil, of basic reality. Jesus uses humility (*humilitas*) to cure the man's unjustifiable blind superiority.

It takes courage to accept your own earthiness and humanity and to reconcile yourself with the fact that you have been made from common clay, like everyone else. Jesus smears dirt on the eyes of the man born blind to tell him: "You will only see things as they really are if you are prepared to confront the common ordinary dirt in yourself and learn to accept it." But Jesus doesn't pound away in an attempt to hammer the truth into the man. He lovingly spreads the mixture of earth and saliva over the man's eyes. Saliva is a motherly substance. The blind man is able to open his eyes and see himself as he really is, only because Jesus treats him in a motherly and tender way. Humility cures pride (*humilitas* heals *hybris*, to use two key terms of the psychology of classical antiquity which are still valid today).

Humility is not only related to *humus*, earth, but to humour. You need humour to accept yourself. Most arrogant and superior people are quite humourless. Woe betide anyone who pokes fun at them, or tries to take them down a peg or two! Jesus also heals the man born blind by treating him humorously. He helps him to come to terms with his humanity by showing him that he has to accept himself with good humour or, as we sometimes say, with equanimity.

I have mentioned a few of the examples of inadequate self-esteem described in the Bible. In fact, all the healing stories in the Bible are about people with minimal self-respect. For instance, there is the leper, the outsider who can't bear himself. Because he doesn't accept himself, he feels rejected and marginalized by everyone else (Mark 1:40-5). There is also the woman who has had a haemorrhage for twelve years and has gone through a great deal at the hands of many doctors, spending all her money in the process, just to get attention. "She had derived no benefit from them but, on the contrary was getting worse" (Mark 5:25-34). Then there is Jairus' daughter, who can't trust in herself enough to stay alive, doesn't want to grow up, and can't assert herself in front of her parents (Mark 5:21-4, 35-43). And there is the man who is deaf and unable to speak intelligibly out of fear that people would reject and make fun of him because of what he might say. He has closed his ears because he is afraid of hearing something detrimental about himself (Mark 7:31-7).

There is also the boy who "has a dumb spirit." Wherever he is, "it gets hold of him, throws him down on the ground and there he foams at the mouth and grinds his teeth. It's simply wearing him out," his father says. The boy actually can't express his feelings. He is driven to and fro by his pent-up aggressiveness, because his father doesn't believe in him (Mark 9:14-29). And, of course, there is the young man of Nain, who is longing to live in a really meaningful way, but somehow just can't manage it (Luke 7:11-7).

When these people meet Jesus, he gives them the courage to stand up for and as themselves, to accept themselves, to hold their heads up, and discover their true worth. Jesus is able to show them that they are worthwhile and unique by what he says to them, by looking at them lovingly, and by touching them tenderly. When he does this, he shows us all ways of helping each other to find our actual value and to believe in it.

3. Learning self-confidence

There are several different ways of developing healthy self-confidence and self-esteem. Psychological methods are always to the fore, and you will find many of them suggested in the wide range of help-books now available. There are also the methods we find in the Bible. In fact the New Testament describes a whole system of self-therapy that Jesus used to help people toward effective self-respect. I shall examine only a few of these methods here. They seem to me the most important because they combine the psychological and spiritual approaches.

Self-acceptance

We cannot face the outside world confidently unless we have some awareness of our unquestionable worth and accept our own uniqueness.

Nowadays, it is scarcely novel to be told that we have to accept ourselves. The problem is how exactly we are to go about it. First of all we have to free ourselves from our illusions about ourselves. We have to say goodbye to the daydreams in which we entertain fantasies of ourselves and make-believe that we are the greatest, the most beautiful person who ever lived. Accepting yourself has something to do with humility, with the courage to accept your own humanity.

Many advisers tell people with inadequate self-esteem that they should concentrate on their strengths. That is often absolutely right. But if the thought behind it is that only strong points count, that advice won't take you any farther. What is decisive is to accept yourself not only with all your good points, but with all your inadequacies. I think the only people with healthy self-esteem are those who also admit that they are weak and inadequate, and can look at their own weaknesses with humour and tolerance.

But we frequently have to follow a long and wearisome path on the way to accepting everything we find in ourselves. The more intensely we live with other people, the more clearly we begin to see our shadow side: our repressed needs and suppressed emotions. A married couple I knew, who were very enthusiastic and confident about building a successful marriage on a basis of shared faith and common endeavour, ruefully discovered after six months or so that they quarrelled more than they had realized was possible, and told me that they were amazed at the number of things they had found they disliked in one another. But for them faith was just another way of evading their own reality. Before they could truly share their lives they had first to learn, slowly and in all humility, to accept the shadow aspects of themselves. They had to learn to accept the pleasure in hurting someone else, the desire for revenge, and all the nastiness of which they were capable.

We can never claim that we have totally accepted ourselves. It is a lifelong process. We constantly discover offensive aspects of our own selves that we never suspected were there.

The older I become the less inclined I am to talk about having accepted myself. When I entered the monastery I thought I had got rid of all my negative features by prayer and asceticism. But then they started to show themselves again, repeatedly. Now I have surrendered the illusory belief that I can ever be the person I would like to be. Now I do my best to say Yes to what is really there, in the certainty that God accepts me however I am. When I constantly get annoyed with myself for having reacted so childishly to someone or something, I tell myself: "Well, that's how I am. That's the way it is." Of course I'm disappointed with myself, but in the midst of my disappointment I begin to feel an inner peace and the conviction that what I essentially am is what I am meant to be, and I know that I am held in God's loving hand.

Accepting yourself means coming to terms with your own life-history. Many people complain that they had a ghastly childhood and were wounded for life. Certainly, when I counsel severely damaged people, having to examine these psychic injuries together is often a very painful process. Some people feel they are under a certain pressure to work through it all as quickly as possible. I try to show these hurt people that their life-history is also their capital, and that it can prove profitable in the years to come. If they can only come to terms with their wounds they will find they are potentially life-giving rather than ugly scars. They can make their own injuries means of understanding others and helping them too. When they try this, people often discover an unsuspected vocation. They come to realize that their supposedly disadvantaged background actually makes them charismatic and healing individuals for many others.

If people manage to reconcile themselves with their own lives, they will also begin to see that everything has a meaning. Even that dreadful weight in the past had a meaning to it. Now it can help them to live differently: more sensitively, more intensely, more thankfully and more openly as far as others are concerned. As soon as they are reconciled with their wounds, they become potentially beneficial not only for their own future lives but for those of countless others too.

To accept yourself, you have to stop comparing yourself with others. As long as I keep comparing myself with him or her, I am at a disadvantage. There are always talents and abilities that others have and I don't. When I compare myself with someone else I am not at peace with myself, but always living in an uneasy state of comparison with others. I have to feel at home in my own skin, accept myself, and like being myself. But if people have too little self-respect, they are inclined to compare and contrast whether they want to or not.

A woman in one of my groups knew very well that this was the worst thing she could do. But as soon as she sat down with a group, the fatal impulse to compare came over her. Then it was no use concentrating on her own good points and praising herself silently. She was still comparing. It didn't help to start criticizing the others, telling herself that what they seemed so good at was all show. She was merely devaluing them in order to elevate her own worth. She was still stuck in the morass of comparison.

It is much more effective to leave the mind, which can't help comparing and discriminating, and to move to the heart, the centre of feeling. When the woman in question did that she found a way of escaping her disastrous impulse to do herself or others down. She tried to feel herself breathing, to be aware of her hands, and so on: to be conscious of herself in and with the person she was. Suddenly she was confident enough to say something when she wanted to. She was no longer under the pressure of having to make some kind of contribution to the group in order to make a good impression on the others. But as long as she compared herself with them she felt uneasy, because the others decided her mood and attitude. When she became conscious of herself as who she truly was, she found this self-awareness enabled her to see and respond to the others as individuals, and to experience true fellowship with them.

Self-awareness

Self-confidence, then, can also mean being self-aware, feeling at home with yourself, and feeling that you are you, there, in your very own skin. It can mean feeling that you are all right as the person you are, quite independently of anyone else.

Many people never develop self-esteem because they give others too much power over them. They are not living in and as themselves. Instead they are always with and around others. They are not at rest in themselves but obtain their self-awareness solely from others: from others' goodwill, praise, kindness and affirmation. They are unable to demarcate themselves from other people. They lack self-definition. As a result, strange to say, they refer everything to themselves and are wounded by the slightest sharp remark. I advise people like this to come to terms with their aggressive impulses.

I can use aggression to define myself in relation to others. Aggression is the impulse to distance myself from others, in order to give myself space to be in and with myself. Sometimes you have to eject the person who has wounded you. As long as I am taken up, occupied as it were, by someone else, I cannot be secure in myself, and I cannot develop self-awareness and self-respect. My life is lived by others, so to speak, whereas I ought to live my own life.

Being inwardly secure, being in and with yourself, can take different forms. I am self-aware when I have a sense of who I am, when I trust my own feelings, and when I am at peace in and with myself. I am not dependent on the mood and attitude of others, but I am in touch with my own emotions. I am self-aware when I feel at home in my own body. For example, if I go for a walk through the woods and the sheer physical effort makes me sweat, then I am at ease with myself. I am in my own body and aware of it. I can feel my body and feel all right in it. I certainly don't start to doubt my own worth. Because I feel, I am. I don't have to demonstrate my value by outward show and achievements. I can feel at home with myself. And that is a good feeling. No one else can feel the way I feel. I am unique. I am myself. This isn't an intellectual discovery but an experience of my own unique value and worth.

Too many people are inclined to look for the causes of their problems in other people. They have to learn how to be in and with themselves, at home with their own selves; to discover the foundations of their own being; and to develop the ability to get in touch with, and remain in touch with, themselves, their feelings and their own bodies.

Knowing your body

A major way of achieving self-awareness and getting the true measure of yourself is to know your own body.

In the 1970s, together with a number of my fellow monks, I often visited Count Dürckheim. He was a well-known Zen master and an expert on the practice of eastern religions. He had written several books on them and on related subjects. Dürckheim taught us how to contact ourselves in and through our bodies. He showed us how to discover our bodies as a way to self-assurance but also to greater openness to God. He showed us how to practise this awareness so that it gradually became more natural and more profound.

For Dürckheim the body was an instrument of human growth. He was absolutely right. The body is a barometer from which you can read off people's real state of being. When people are unsure and lack self-confidence, they always betray this in their attitudes to their bodies. Watch them and you will see, for instance, that they are physically as well as emotionally uptight. They draw themselves up into unnatural positions. They can't let their arms hang freely. They walk around in a cramped posture, as if trying to get a hold on themselves. They put all their energy into making sure that they are actually still there.

Other people draw their shoulders up into an equally unrelaxed position, because they're full of panic fear. Many people who lack self-assurance act as if they were entirely focussed on their chest area. They're never at ease with themselves. They fix themselves in awkward positions so that they look tough and hard-boiled to the outside world (or so they think). The truth is they are totally insecure. So insecure that if you leaned over and pressed them lightly with your finger they would topple over immediately.

The body is not only a barometer but an instrument of self-development, in more than the physical sense. I can work through my body to practise and achieve certain inner attitudes and states of mind as well as body. For example, training myself to stand properly can help me not only to stand in a relaxed yet confident way, but to reach overall self-confidence—of body and of soul.

For instance, I might imagine myself standing here like a tree. Here I am: I am a tree. My roots thrust deep down into this earth below me. I know that I can withstand wind and storm if I am deep-rooted. I know I am really well-rooted when my weight is concentrated between my heels and the balls of my feet. Let me try flexing my knees slightly without moving from the spot. Yes, I can do that and remain as firmly based as a tree. After all, I am a tree, not a concrete pillar.

As I breathe out, I imagine my breath passing down through the soles of my feet and into the ground. When I breathe in, it rises up out of the earth and passes through my cranium until it reaches the sky above me. I am a tree deeply rooted below and opening its crown out to the heavens above. I stand like this, secure yet open, and feel my self-confidence growing as I grow. I tell myself: "I can stand securely. I have both feet on the ground. I know where I stand. I can stand up to things. I can stand up for myself and for my ideas and beliefs. I can stand firm and secure in myself."

Or, as I stand like that, firm and secure as a tree, I can repeat some sayings from the Bible: "Cast your burden on the Lord, and he will sustain you" (Ps. 55:23); or: "I keep the Lord always before me; because he is at my right hand, I shall not be moved" (Ps. 16:8). I learn (and constantly repeat the discovery) that I cannot find self-respect and self-confidence through reason alone. Meditation with the body can help me to grow more self-assured. Of course, it isn't some kind of trick that will switch my confidence on, hey-presto!—just like that. I have to practise it constantly.

Dürckheim said that we should stand firm in the state known as *hara*. If I think of my central point as located in my hypogastric region—the lower middle area of my abdomen—I shall feel secure. If my weight is concentrated there, it is much more difficult for anyone to push me over. Being in *hara* doesn't mean thinking of yourself as immovable because you are forcibly implanted or rammed into the ground, so that however hard people shove, you can't be knocked over. *Hara* certainly offers security, but it is essentially openness and even permeability. I don't hold on to myself grimly and constrain myself to resist all onslaughts, but make myself open to God, or to existence, or (as Dürckheim always said) to being. This openness gives me a profound sense of security. Because I am open to something greater than myself, I do not tighten myself up in an attempt to contain myself within myself. Instead I sense God holding and supporting me.

When I lecture or talk to groups, and I am consciously in *hara*, I become calm and clear. Many people stand in a rigid, fixed position on the platform when they address an audience, or they rock from one foot to the other, showing their insecurity and, in fact, reinforcing it. Explicitly placing yourself in a state of *hara* means practising trust, confidence, and openness. I am not seeking to impress people by what I have to say, but trying to allow something greater than me to permeate me and others through me, in the hope that God will address people through me.

Many people think that there is no remedy for a "natural" lack of self-confidence. But we are not simply condemned to suffer in this way. We can slowly train our bodies to help us grow more self-assured. Of course this process of transformation through the body is gradual. It demands considerable patience. And the body won't allow itself simply to be used for this or that purpose: merely to make myself more self-assured, for example. My body asks for honesty and integrity. *Hara* means being permeable to what is greater than us. It means openness to God. Authentic self-confidence can develop through our bodies only if we abandon absolute adherence to our own yardsticks and demands. We have to be prepared to cast off from our own rigid selves and to entrust ourselves to God, who alone offers true security and guarantees our individual dignity and value.

Knowing your faith

Ultimately, I think, self-respect is a religious question. Faith can show us who we actually are, and where we obtain our true value. But it is not enough simply to tell people that if they want to be self-confident, all they have to do is to trust in God. The real question is how we can learn to trust in God. Telling people to trust in him doesn't make them confident.

Pious people often find themselves in a dead-end situation because they feel guilty about their lack of trust in God. They think they are probably not praying sufficiently or with enough intensity. So they try praying more and more, and more emotionally, in a desperate attempt to drive themselves into a state of trust in God. But, however often, and however intensely they pray, they repeatedly find themselves in situations where they lack self-confidence. Prayer and self-reproach follow one another in a never-ending, pointless sequence.

You can't use prayer to make yourself trust in God. But you can acquire that confidence by keeping in mind the trust that God has in you, and by training yourself to trust in him. It is the work of grace, a gift, when profound trust in God does develop in you, and that reliance produces new self-confidence. I find it helpful simply to behave as if I trust in him. For instance, I take some words of comfort from the Bible and recite them, then try acting as if their implications were obvious matters of fact. For example, if I keep repeating Psalm 118: "With the Lord on my side I do not fear. What can mortals do to me?" these words keep me in contact with the trust that is certainly already there, deep within me. Jung says that we all exist on a continuum between the two poles of fear and confidence. We always have both fear and confidence inside us. There is no one who is only subject to fear; and no one who is supremely confident. Too often, however, we are fixated on our fear. Consolatory words from scripture help to contact the confidence that is there in the very depths of our souls. The more we contact it, the more room it has to grow in us, and the more it becomes a healthy and conscious part of our lives. When I meditate on Psalm 23: "The Lord is my shepherd, I shall not want," the more surely I shall know that this is fact and not sheer fancy. Of course, from time to time I shall still wonder whether the sentiment isn't too fine and beautiful to be true. No matter. When I meditate I think and act, there, inside myself, as if the statement were absolutely, unmistakably true. I practise taking it as absolute, guaranteed, well-proven fact. As I "practise" the truth in this way, I allow a feeling of freedom from other people to grow in me. I allow my independence of them to develop inside me. I sense, then grow into, the conviction that God is sufficient for me; that he will give me what I need; and that he has given me, and maintains, my true dignity and worth.

The basis of our faith is that God accepts us unconditionally. When we were baptized God told us: "You are my beloved son, you are my beloved daughter, in whom I am well pleased" (cf. Mark 1:11). If I live on the basis of this fact, many of my fears and doubts about myself will disappear, and the negative messages I have heard so often ("You're worthless! You'll never manage it! You're too stupid!") will fade away.

The real question is how we are to live on this basis of faith so that it fills and shapes us more than our negativity towards ourselves; more surely than all the accusations and insults we usually heap on ourselves. Two major ways of progressing in this respect are meditation on biblical texts and celebrating Christian feasts.

Meditating on the Bible

I set some people suffering from lack of self-esteem individual exercises in meditation on texts from the Bible that I think are specially relevant to them, and will help to make them confident and discover their own value. Every page of the Old and New Testaments assures us that we have an unassailable dignity and worth. If we believe in our God-given value we can build a healthy self-awareness and free ourselves from slavery to other people's opinions. One text that can help us to trust in God's protection, and to acknowledge our worth on the basis of that trust, is Isaiah 43: "Do not fear, for I have redeemed you; I have called you by name, you are mine. When you pass through the waters, I will be with you; and through the rivers, they shall not overwhelm you; when you walk through fire you shall not be burned, and the flame shall not consume you. . . . Because you are precious in my sight, and honoured, and I love you. I give people in return for you, nations in exchange for your life" (Isa. 43:2ff). I do not merely read these words with my rational mind but let them drop into my heart. I try to sense their unmistakable reality: "If that is really true, how should I feel? If that is the ultimate truth about me, what do I mean to myself?" I have to repeat the words again and again and assure myself: "Yes, that is the real truth. It is more real than any feelings you have about yourself, and more real than any self-assessment." Then I may begin to sense the beginnings of confidence that God is with me and that I definitely am worth something; that I am so valuable to God that he would sacrifice entire countries for my sake. Water—all the threats and dangers in my unconscious self—cannot bear me down; nor can the fire of my emotions and impulses consume me. I need have no fear of any menace outside or inside me. God is with me.

I always find that meditating on texts like that helps people lacking self-respect to discover their true value. I constantly come across people who run themselves down, and declare that they are inadequate because they can't behave as if they trusted in God or themselves. They know, they say, that they ought to be confident. Intellectually, or because they've been told so, they realize there is no reason to be afraid, and they ought to have no worries, for of course there is a God, and he must be supporting them somehow. They know they are at fault here, they keep repeating, because they should behave as if that were true. But rational assertions of any kind are not much use. All statements beginning "I know I should . . ." at best serve only to reinforce guilt feelings, because people just are anxious and afraid, even though they realize there is no reason to be. You can't force trust and you can't build confidence by insisting that people should be rational, get a grip on themselves, look at the facts, and so on. Trust is a gradual process. Self-confidence grows. It has to penetrate and reshape the unconscious. It can grow if I so to speak taste and chew over the word of God, if I let it sink deeper and deeper into me. Then it will gradually transform me, as trust and assurance slowly gather in my real self.

I often suggest meditating on Isaiah 54: "Sing aloud, O barren woman who never bore a child, break into cries of joy, you who have never been in labour; for the deserted wife has more sons than she who lives in wedlock, says the Lord. Enlarge the limits of your home, spread wide the curtains of your tent, let out its ropes to the full and drive the pegs home!" (Isa. 54:1ff).

Perhaps I feel unfruitful and lonely. I feel that I am useless, that my life has been pointless to date, and that everything is worthless and meaningless. If I let these words of God drop into that dry and barren state of mind, then my self-reproaches and self-castigation will often fade away or even vanish. I may indeed be barren, and sometimes I do feel totally alone and abandoned. But then I am the very person who needs that encouragement and promise. They are meant for me. I am the very person whose life can bring forth a rich harvest. Spreading the curtains of my tent means that I have to realize the full extent of my inner space. I mustn't make myself too small. I do not need to belittle myself. My heart is infinitely spacious. I can open out to the love and promise of God, who will create the space I need to be myself and to develop. Not only that. There is enough room in my inner home to invite other people in. My tent is truly capacious. God has given me a wonderful home where he himself has chosen to live, there inside me. I have no need to hide. I must have faith in my inner beauty and invite other people in to rejoice with me over the personal glory and wonder that God has certainly endowed me with.

When meditating on biblical texts, I never try to force anything from myself or others. Appeals to the moral law don't count for much. God himself has told me that. They merely reinforce a guilty conscience, which is destructive of true faith. Meditation is a sensitive, calm, and gentle route to truth. As I hear and sense the atmosphere and meaning of the words of scripture, I let God himself act on my spirit. I offer myself and my inadequate self-respect to God so that he can suffuse me with his Word, with his Spirit, and with his love.

In the kind of spiritual exercises I have in mind it is not a matter of solving your problems but of letting yourself be transformed by God. At the same time, if you truly sense your divine beginnings, that is, that God has made and is now remaking you, you will begin to tackle your everyday difficulties in a different way. There is no need to force yourself to be self-confident. You know that you possess inner depths, a God-given value, and a unique image that God has given to you alone.

Celebrating feasts

The feasts of the church year are special ways of meditating on the message of the Bible. When we celebrate these feasts we also celebrate our own lives, which were made by "Almighty God, who wonderfully created us in your own image and yet more wonderfully restored us through your Son, Jesus Christ" (Christmas collect from the Alternative Service Book of the Church of England). We celebrate our lives because they are worth celebrating. In the liturgy we symbolically enact our existence as redeemed human beings. We are involved in a sacred drama, a form of play that helps us to see who we really are and encourages our sense of our unique value.

At Christmas, for example, we celebrate the birth of God in our hearts. God is born in us as a child. Our past doesn't determine us for ever. God enables us to make a new start. He puts us in touch with the genuine image that he made of us in the first place. Because I can't trust in my own worth, and because I continually devalue myself, as Christ is born God himself comes to me with the sole purpose of reassuring me: "You are wonderful and beautiful and unique." At Christmas we celebrate the divine beauty that radiates from the Child of Bethlehem to touch us all individually, and, as it does so, shines out from every human face.

At Christmas three powerful images reflect the mystery of our redeemed existence. One is the birth of Christ in my manger. The light of God illumines my darkness and transforms the chaos in my heart. We celebrate this event in the Holy Night of Christmas. I don't have to put any kind of show on for God. All I need do is keep the manger of my self ready for him, and his light will shine there.

Epiphany is concerned with the appearance of God's glory in my body. We gave a course on this feast once in our centre, and spent much of the time concentrating on the divine glory in our bodies. Our exercise was to try to realize what that really means for each of us. How do I feel, what do I mean for myself, how do I experience myself if that really is (and it is) the most profound aspect of my being? As our guests became more deeply involved in the mystery of this feast, they developed a new sense of their own presence and value that transformed the whole occasion. It is no exaggeration to say that everyone there grew more beautiful to behold as they became aware that they were more glorious within.

We celebrate the third image in the feast of Jesus' baptism, which closes the Christmas period. As Jesus stands in the middle of the River Jordan, the heavens split open above him and he hears the voice of God saying: "You are my dearly-beloved Son, with whom I am well pleased" (Mark 1:11). The waters of Jordan are full of the guilt of all the sinners whom John has baptized there. I, too, stand there, in the midst of my guilt, and the heavens open above me, too. My life widens out until it extends into the divine realm itself, into the very depths of Heaven. And God himself talks to me from those depths, pronouncing for me with the utmost clarity the basic message of my irreducible dignity and worth: "You are my beloved son, my beloved daughter, with whom I am well pleased." Being the son or daughter of God gives me my divine value. I can stop defining myself in terms of my parents or what they say. I do not derive my worth from other people, neither from my father nor from my mother, not from their attention and assurance, but from God. I do not receive my real value from other people's praise and support but from the fact that God has made me so wonderful and extraordinary. Being born of God liberates me from the expectations and judgements of human beings. Jesus Christ, the Son of God, became human so that I could be God's son or daughter; so that I could be "divinized," as the Greek Fathers of the Church put it.

The image that God has made of each of us, the divine value that he has given us in Jesus Christ, gradually becomes more evident as the church year unfolds. In Lent we train ourselves to learn more about our inner freedom, so that we are not dependent on our habits. These exercises will reinforce our self-respect. We are not determined from outside but shape our own lives. Fasting can help to make the body more sensitive to God's presence and lead to a more intense life. Then we become more aware of ourselves and of the world around us. Sensible fasting can make us more attentive and alert. St Augustine said that fasting prepares our bodies for the resurrection.

At Easter we celebrate not only Jesus' resurrection but our own revival. Every year about 250 young people come to our abbey to celebrate Easter with the community. They realize that it is a feast concerned with their own resurrection, with their remaking, and that in the resurrection of Jesus God has broken their chains. They come to see that he has rolled away the stones that weighed so heavily on them and stopped them living effectively, and that he wants to show them the way out of their tomblike existence—the way that leads to a new life. They celebrate the victory of life over death. They stand up, and sing and dance, in order to resist all the forces that prevent us living authentically. They stand up straight to celebrate the conquest of death by life, and the victory of love over hatred. They allow Christ to raise them up from the grave of their fears and hopelessness, so that they can stand up to celebrate their dignity and value as redeemed and liberated human beings. Many young people have told me that celebrating Easter with such intensity and feeling has had a profound effect on them. They find that it gives them a real sense of empowerment, and helps them to live with conviction the lives of people who know that they are truly worthwhile.

Pentecost completes the Easter process of rising and standing up to be new people. The Holy Spirit enables the scared apostles to go out into the world to proclaim the resurrection of Jesus. The Spirit transforms these frightened people into self-confident apostles. They begin to trust in themselves, knowing that they can advance with their heads held high, for they sense the divine fire that burns in them and can empower their lives with new enthusiasm.

I meet many young people who don't trust their own feelings. They are particularly liable to feel downcast when others make them feel guilty. I'm thinking here of the kind of people who tell them that Christian morality demands an obviously strict observance of their faith in the face of the world. But the Holy Spirit speaks to us with a quiet voice. The fire of Pentecost is an inner fire that encourages us to listen to this inner voice, to trust our own emotions, and to shun the attempts of moralists to scare us into supposedly good behaviour. The Holy Spirit is in us. He speaks to us individually. He is not an outsider who demands or forces us to do something, but the Spirit we know, the Spirit within who keeps us in touch with the divine image that is always there inside us. When we pray quietly and calmly we often hear the Spirit talking to us. He never frightens us but gently leads us towards the truth that makes us free. He shows us who we really are. If we trust the Spirit in our own hearts, we shall prove all the more surely that we are the unique individuals God intended us to be.

The feasts of the church year are designed to show us how God helps us to remake ourselves through Jesus' saving power. They are images of our redemption and of the value we have for God. This is also true of the commemorations of the saints. They show how each person is a unique expression of God, a different way by which God can indeed be seen in this world. This is true of the feasts of Mary, which are always optimistic, and intended to encourage women to assert their real value and dignity. Unfortunately some groups and people in the Church misuse the figure of Our Lady to make women feel guilty and dissatisfied with themselves. Mary has been placed on so high a pedestal that all other women must surely feel devalued in comparison with this lofty ideal. But that is not the real meaning of the feasts of Mary. When we celebrate them, we celebrate our own salvation. We commemorate what God has done to and for us in Jesus Christ. Take the Annunciation, for instance. It shows Mary as a model of faith: as a courageous woman who, contrary to what everyone else might expect, makes her own decision to trust in God. The world around her may ignore God, but she remains confident. She trusts in God and trusts in herself: "I belong to the Lord, body and soul. Let it happen as you say" (Luke 1:38). She is a very young woman from Nazareth, which means from nowhere of any importance. But she dares to speak up for herself, for her nation, for all humanity, and says she is ready to do and be what her God-given uniqueness can do and be.

The liturgy is full of extraordinarily powerful metaphors, or word-pictures that convey the mystery of this woman whom God chose to bear his Son. But they also convey the value, uniqueness and beauty of each and every one of us. They declare that we, too, are called to experience the same mystery, for God wants to be born in us as well. The liturgy has always maintained a theology that is fascinatingly different from the official Church's view of women. In the Marian feasts it places women at the centre: the woman through whom Christ was born and through whom redemption entered this world. Feminist theology is only now beginning to rediscover the implications of the liturgical understanding of Mary and the true dignity of being a woman.

The Pauline way

In his letters, Paul repeatedly tells us that Christ has freed us from any dependence on other people and their opinions: "All who follow the leading of God's Spirit are God's own sons. Nor are you meant to relapse into the old slavish attitude of fear—you have been adopted into the very family circle of God and you can say with a full heart, 'Father, my Father!'"(Rom. 8:14ff).

For Paul, the most important aspect of being the sons and daughters of God is liberation from slavery by human beings. A slave is subject to human power and fears other people. Symbolically, a "slave" is also anyone who lets other people have power over him or her. Slaves are people who allow their self-esteem to be governed by what other people say and do. They feel positive if others take notice of them. If they are rejected, their little world collapses.

I allow others to have power over me if I make myself dependent on their mood or attitude. There are some people whose feelings depend entirely on whomsoever they live with or spend their time with. If the others are annoyed, they are discouraged or even completely crushed. If the others seem depressed, then they become sad or feel guilty.

But we are sons and daughters of God and not slaves of human beings. We must never surrender ourselves totally to someone else, or put ourselves in his or her hands. We must never give other people power over us. If we do that, we live in constant fear that they will misuse that power to wound and destroy us. For Paul, being sons and daughters of God is the opposite of being afraid. God gives us our true value, which no one can take away from us. Other people can certainly do us an injury, but there is a permanent dignity and value in us that no one can rob us of.

It is helpful for those who are depressed and anxious about their own inadequacies and faults to remember how Paul felt when he said: "I have cheerfully made up my mind to be proud of my weaknesses, because they mean a deeper experience of the power of Christ. I can even enjoy weaknesses, suffering, privations, persecutions and difficulties for Christ's sake. For my very weakness makes me strong in him" (2 Cor. 12:10). Self-confidence doesn't mean that we are always strong and can surmount every problem, that we can resolve every problematical aspect of our character and life all on our own. We show our self-confidence if we bear up in the midst of our weakness because we believe in the grace of God, which can support us and enable us to be worthwhile human beings in spite of all our inadequacies.

If your self-respect depends on always being strong and fulfilling all your ideals, the experience of failure and weakness will inevitably bring you down. But if you admit that you can be weak you will grow in inner strength. Disappointments and failures will not sap your self-respect, because you know that God still cares for you. You will draw your value and self-empowerment from the same faith that Paul describes when he says: "I have become absolutely convinced that neither death nor life, neither messenger of Heaven nor monarch of earth, neither what happens today nor what may happen tomorrow, neither a power from on high nor a power from below, nor anything else in God's whole world has any power to separate us from the love of God in Christ Jesus our Lord!" (Rom. 8:38).

Reconciliation

One of the central messages in the Bible is the news that reconciliation is possible. When Paul writes: "God was in Christ personally reconciling the world to himself—not counting their sins against them—and has commissioned us with the message of reconciliation. . . . As [Christ's] personal representatives we say: 'Make your peace with God'" (2 Cor. 5:20), he refers to being reconciled to and with ourselves and to and with other people. Jesus wants those who are inwardly at war with themselves to be at peace with themselves when he tells them that God accepts them in spite of all their guilt. But this means that when God forgives them and stops blaming them, they have to stop blaming themselves as well. Trust in God's forgiveness also means forgiving yourself. There is no point now in blaming yourself and cosseting your guilt-feelings. The forgiveness that Christ not only told people about but offered in his own person and behaviour enables us to be reconciled with, to come to terms with, and to forgive ourselves and our past lives.

I no longer have to shut my eyes to what I've done wrong. I know that it is forgiven, and that it no longer separates me from God or from myself and other people. Guilt means division. People who feel guilty feel inwardly divided. Their self-respect is uncertain, minimal or non-existent. They have lost meaningful contact with themselves and their real inner selves.

When Jesus promises people that God will forgive them, he gives them the courage to put themselves together again, to stand up and make a new start. He tells the paralyzed man whose sins he forgives to "Stand up, pick up your bed, and walk!" He tells him not to let his past life paralyze him. The fact that he has piled all that guilt on his own shoulders is not a sufficient reason for refusing to live.

Jesus trusts the woman caught in adultery to make a new beginning. He says: "Neither do I condemn you. Go home and do not sin again" (John 8:11). Forgiveness makes it possible to begin again straightaway. Jesus issues a challenge to the woman and also strengthens her weak ego. He doesn't humiliate her by moralizing or by weighing her down with the burden of the law, but straightens her up by trusting her to live a worthwhile life. She didn't fall into sin out of sheer lust, or because she was looking for pleasure at any cost, but because she simply couldn't say No. She did what she did because she was confused and wasn't at ease with herself. Jesus addresses her real self: "You can live a different kind of life. You have the strength to do it. Try living differently. You will see that it's right for you." Jesus doesn't ask the woman to be submissive but supports her, and helps her to be her own person, by addressing the power he knows she has in her, and the individual dignity and worth she really wants to live up to.

We can release the underlying self-confidence in people by showing them that we trust them in some way. This is also evident in Jesus' encounter with the "woman, known as a bad woman," in Luke 7. When Jesus has forgiven her sins he says: "It is your faith that has saved you. Go in peace" (Luke 7:50). Jesus praises her faith. He reinforces the positive things the woman has done and helps her to be aware of her power for good. He shows that he trusts her: "Go in peace! Don't burden yourself with guilt. What has happened has happened. Now you can go in peace: in peace with yourself and in peace with other people. You don't have to make excuses for being as you are. You are a worthwhile person. You have the capacity for peace. In fact, you are brimming with all the potential for a complete and fulfilled life. Now go and live it!"

In their pastoral work, the early Christian monks followed Jesus' practice here. They encouraged and showed their confidence in the pupils who asked them for advice by suggesting a way of life or certain curative as well as symbolic practices, saying, "Go on, do it!," and trusting them actually to go ahead and try it. One of them advised a disciple not to talk for a whole year. He recommended that another should eat only every second day. By giving a clear directive, and then leaving it to his followers to try the new way of life for themselves, their spiritual guide strengthened their self-confidence. The pupils needed the instruction, but then discovered what they were capable of, grew more adept, and enjoyed their life because they were working it out for themselves on the basis of helpful advice.

I follow the same method myself. I find more is needed than a non-directive conversation, however useful that might be as a first step towards self-assurance. I realized long ago that I have to go further. As often as not I have to challenge people to act in some way. There has to be a specific effort to make, before they can make an effort. They need a challenge to enable them to start flexing the muscles of moral, spiritual, and creative enterprise. They need it in order to discover their capabilities, and so that their personal power can begin to emerge and flourish. So I often give people an appropriate exercise. I suggest, say, praying out loud, talking to God openly for an hour, so that they can pour out all their pent-up feelings and thoughts. Or I ask them to write a letter. I ask them to imagine that they've been told there's only a short time to go before they die. They decide to write to someone for the last time and tell him or her what they tried to do in their lives, and what their guiding principles were. Of course some people resist or refuse these "tasks." But whenever they decide to go ahead with them, the results are positive.

Naturally, there's no question of ordering people to do things. There's a nice balance to be observed here. Non-directive (or "client-centred") counselling tries to encourage personal growth strictly through self-definition and seeks to provide a warm, "permissive" setting that is so sympathetic, and where the therapist is so empathetic (so understands and reflects clients' attitudes), that people will "naturally" take the direction that is "naturally" good for and true to each of them. Any kind of diagnosis or technique is de-emphasized in favour of a sometimes vague "right kind of attitude" on the counsellor's part. Non-directiveness is certainly to be recommended when it really does enable people to discover their actual capacities by themselves, and they're definitely the sort of people who are probably going to do that anyway. But I'm always very sceptical about any method of counselling or therapy that claims to be the only valid one, the unique cure-all. Experience has shown me that the counterpart of non-directive counselling is also important, and that active encouragement and a challenge are necessary to reinforce people's self-esteem and self-confidence.

Challenging people to go forward doesn't mean humiliating them. It certainly doesn't mean offering the kind of advice that only too often amounts to a psychic slap across the face. It means a suggestion: proposing a way of practising that in no way harms individual freedom and dignity. It means suggesting how people can train themselves to discover and develop their own powers and capabilities.

Jesus confronts and challenges people because he believes that they are essentially good. When I am acting as a priest and pastor, challenge people, and propose an exercise or method of self-training, I do so because I believe in the Holy Spirit who is at work in those people and longs to evoke or release new and unsuspected potentialities in them. Jesus brings those whom he addresses in such a direct and confrontational way into contact with the power of the Spirit at work in them. He opens their eyes to the fact that God wants them to do more than be satisfied with things as they are. Jesus wakes people up. He shocks them into realizing that the Spirit is there inside them, and is actually moving in them. He shows them how to detect and realize the possibilities of the original, unique images that God has given them.

The mystical way

The mystical way is another method of building up effective self-esteem. Mystics—like practitioners of transpersonal psychology—believe that there is a space within us to which other people cannot gain access, and which the considerations of the super-ego cannot reach or affect. This is the quiet space, the realm of quietude, where God himself dwells in us. Where God lives within us other people can have no power over us. Mystics believe that every single one of us has such a space deep inside him or her. Many people, however, never realize that they have this area within them, because they are cut off from it by a stratum of rubbish and rubble. This is a layer packed with worries and problems, thoughts and plans, that have intervened between their conscious minds and their real selves.

The way to that inner area of silence is the way of prayer and meditation. In the monastic life, a method has been developed over many years that uses single words and phrases or simple sentences to begin this journey towards the inner self. You simply associate a saying from Scripture, such as "Behold, I am with you!" or the Jesus prayer, "Lord Jesus Christ, Son of God, have mercy on me," with your breath. You focus all your attention on your breathing and join the saying or prayer to the natural process of respiration. As you breathe out the saying, you allow yourself to be taken into that quiet inner space where God dwells within you.

The mystic Isaac of Nineveh says that the saying I meditate on will open the doors to the silent mystery of God, and even to the house of peace to which God alone has access. When I meditate I do not always reach or sense this still and silent realm within me. Often all I have is a fleeting apprehension of the presence of something quite different in me; a transient sense that God himself is there within me. But even this slight encounter with mystery and wonder starts something moving in me. I experience myself in a totally different way. I touch the fringes of my true being. I am on the brink of the profundity that is certainly there within me. I begin to sense the presence of a deep quiet, the source of an extraordinary peace that seems to be emerging and radiating from that strange and wonderful space there within me.

Sometimes it helps just to imagine that quiet place within me, perhaps by using the images that the Bible draws on to describe this still and silent space of wonder. I do not look at these images from the outside, as it were, but I look at myself through them. In the Gospel according to John, Jesus says that those who believe "will have rivers of living water flowing from their inmost heart" (John 7:38). And there is a source in me that never dries up: the ever-flowing spring of the Holy Spirit. To sense it, I can breathe out and, as I do so, imagine myself penetrating the layers of rubbish and waste that I have deposited over this source, until I come to the first unmistakable evidence of this pure spring in the depths of my soul, and sense it forcing its way through and cleansing the troubled waters of my con-fused emotions, until I am inwardly refreshed. Or I can meditate on the image of the living God, the Almighty to whom (as the Letter to Jewish Christians, or to the Hebrews, tells us) only Jesus, the compassionate and faithful High Priest, has access. By meditating on this biblical word-picture I can contact the reality it represents: Jesus Christ, who dwells in me. The noise and tumult in the forecourt of the Temple cannot reach that space where Jesus is within me. The heathen cannot enter that sanctuary. Business, trade and industry, and secular affairs cannot penetrate there. The other priests are forbidden entry. Not even my own worries and plans can disturb me there.

In this inner space I begin to sense who I really am. There I come into contact with my own self. Where God dwells within me, he liberates me from the power of human beings: from their complaints and expectations, from their judgements and the yardsticks by which they measure my competence and worth. There he frees me from the packaging of false images and prejudices others have left me in, or that I have so assiduously wrapped round my real self.

God liberates me to experience my very own self. I am more than my life-history. I am a unique image of God. Within me there is a fresh and untroubled image that God has made of me. This is my true being, as God shaped it.

Meditation also leads me to my authentic self. There, where the opinions of other people and even my own usual standards of judgement have no validity, I can really be myself. There I can apprehend my divine worth. There, in the profundity of my own self, I am in direct contact with God himself.

I constantly meet people who suffer from others determining their thoughts, feelings, and lives in one way or another. They cannot develop anything approaching self-confidence because other people rob them of it. Their fellow workers and the boss are always finding fault with them. A moody neighbour or a frustrated aunt takes out his or her dissatisfaction on them. I try to show these victims of others' problems the way to that peaceful place within them. They have to picture themselves there, in that extraordinary quiet, protected space, and think of themselves as safe from all interference. What the person next door thinks can't affect them there. What others say about them is blocked: all the gossip, whispering, criticism, rejection, demands, and expectations are quite ineffectual there.

On an emotional level, of course, I am still sensitive and affected by others' remarks. But on another level, in that still space where nothing outside can touch me, in the very process of my contemplating it, it becomes reality. I actually feel free. In that space within me I can breathe freely. There no one else can decide what I am. Not even my own expectations of myself, let alone my demands, work targets, appointments and so on, can determine who I am.

Some time ago I gave a course for marriage advisers on spirituality and counselling. I tried to show these psychologists and associated professionals that spirituality in counselling doesn't mean religious or even vaguely pious sentiments but directing people to the core of their authentic being, to their unquestionable dignity and value, and to that peaceful space within them. Some advisers told me when a marriage goes wrong, even practising better methods of communicating between the partners is no use. A wife may feel so deeply wounded that no discussion whatsoever is possible. A husband may feel absolutely rejected, so that he can't bring himself to say a single word to his wife. Then it can be helpful to show one or the other the way to that inner space where the other partner cannot enter, and where hurt and rejection cannot penetrate. There each of them can discover his or her unassailable personal value: the area that remains whole, untouched and secure. Even in the midst of utter rejection and psychic injury, the mere suggestion of this space, the sense that it exists and that there is a worth no one can take away from you, can build a new and growing conviction of empowerment.

One of the most effective ways of freeing myself from people who constantly remove my own sense of self, who wound and worry me, is to cast them out: to eject them from my own self-awareness. Anger can be a positive means of sweeping out people who have power over us, so that our personal space of peace and quiet is really occupied by God alone. There is no way round it. We have to stop some people from gaining entry to our inward realm. They must never be allowed to step over our personal threshold. Where God dwells in us, and where we are at home with God, no other person has the right to enter.

One day I was consulted by a woman who was victimized by the manageress of her department. At home in the evening, at the dinner table, the only subject of conversation was this frightful manageress, who was making life sheer hell for her. I said: "I wouldn't let a spiteful, worthless boss like that dominate or even disturb my meals. She doesn't deserve what amounts to a kind of respect. Don't let her into your house. She isn't that important."

Instead of letting anger eat us up inside, instead of exploding with rage, we should use our anger to distance ourselves from people who steal our time and attention. In fact, we have to eject them altogether. Of course some people might say this isn't Christian behaviour, and that forgiveness—not angry expulsion—is the Christian thing to do. But anger is a process. Forgiveness is its last and not its first stage. As long as the person who has injured me is still in my heart, forgiveness would be no more than masochism. If I forgave him or her I would harm myself. Only when I have distanced myself from him or her can I really forgive that person, knowing that he or she too is only a psychically wounded child.

Ejecting the other person from my own self is only the first step towards learning to know the quiet space within me. It is a means of defending that area from all those who want to occupy it by force. But defence alone is not enough. By meditation I must separate myself inwardly from everything else by which I am preoccupied. I have to cut myself off from the people I give so much attention to, and from my own thoughts and plans. I have to become totally quiet and peaceful, and not preoccupied in any way, but just be there in my own inner quiet. Then I must say to myself: There is a mystery within me that is greater than me. When I withdraw into my inward self I do not merely retreat to the level of contemplating my own past life and my problems. Below that level, deep down within me, is an area of tranquillity and stillness. It is a place where God, the ultimate Mystery, lives within me. I am truly at home where God, the Mystery of mysteries, dwells in this mysterious place inside me. There I can sense profound calm and perfect harmony. I know that there, beneath all the noise and bustle of everyday life, and below all my inward worries and troubles, there is a secure place where peace reigns undisturbed. Evagrius Ponticus, the leading monastic writer of the fourth century, used the image of Jerusalem to describe this secret place. Jerusalem, after all, means "vision of peace." We enter that realm of quiet in order to enjoy the "vision of peace in which a human being can see a peace within himself or herself that surpasses all understanding and protects our hearts from all harm."[12]

When I enter that stillness inside my being, a feeling of freedom and of trust grows in me. This is no mere outward show of self-confidence, constructed for the world to see, but an assurance derived from true inner freedom. It enables me to enjoy my personal freedom, and to forsake pointless, destructive struggle with other people. There is a space within me where no one has power over me, for it is the home of God. There I am in touch with my own true self. There I am entirely who I really am. There my own true self is safe. It is there that my authentic self-esteem is nurtured and I am increasingly one with myself, until I reach the point at which I am indeed me, whole and entire.

All truly religious ways eventually lead us to this point of real self-empowerment. But it is a gradual process. There is no spiritual trick or how-to-do kit that will suddenly make us self-confident and fully empowered. There are only practices and exercises that help us along the way. I must constantly meditate on the word of God until it transforms my heart and drives all anxiety and fear from me. I must pray so that I continually come into contact with the quiet space within me, in order to sense and know that I am independent of others' opinions and of the judgements of my own super-ego. If I follow this way of spiritual practice calmly, honestly, trustingly and attentively, I shall find an authentic feeling of self-confidence growing to fullness in me. I am not simply condemned to live the rest of my life with the mean ration of self-assurance that I acquired as a child. Self-confidence can be learnt.

Faith is an excellent school for learning how to acquire self-confidence and a true conviction of our own dignity and worth. But, like all schools, it demands endurance and practice. And of course faith can't evade psychological reality. As a believer I must try to come to terms with, to be reconciled to, the injuries that have wounded my self-esteem. As a believer I must make use of all the aids that psychology offers me. But faith also provides a way of reaching my authentic self: the me that God intended me to be; the self that he made me to be. In the dimension of faith I pass beyond the psychological level and discover the transpersonal level in myself: the space within me where God dwells and where I am my own true self, whole and entire. When I am in touch with my true self, I have a self-confidence that failure and errors cannot destroy. It is a sense of the divine core of my inner being over which this world has no power.

II Remaking the Real You

This is an age of particularly overwhelming experiences of powerlessness based on political and social conditions. I need mention only powerlessness with regard to injustice in the world, and powerlessness with regard to terrorism, brutality, and war. In the 1960s optimism and hope for the future were essential elements of the contemporary mood, but reversals in economic, political, and social development have brought the dream of unrestricted progress to "an abrupt close. For the young generation especially, trust in a beneficial future and in its sustainability has disappeared. It has been replaced by a general feeling of helplessness with respect to seemingly inevitable objective forces. The result is a tendency to resignation and egocentric withdrawal."[13]

The experience of our own powerlessness is an essential aspect of human life. Freud devoted much of his work to studying powerlessness in children. An infant experiences its dependence on its mother and on things in the external world. This "evokes painful feelings of helplessness, anger and rage."[14] The stage during which a child experiences itself in a state of harmony with its mother and the world is generally followed by "the experience of powerlessness and emotions that are difficult to master, as represented in the myths of the fall of the angels from heaven and the expulsion of humanity from the Garden of Eden."[15] The child's task is to respond to "the experience of its own powerlessness, dependence, lack of value and subordination"[16] by developing a healthy self-awareness and self-confidence. If a child feels that it is helpless with regard to people or its own impulses, it reacts with anxiety and fear. Feelings of powerlessness, self-respect and self-confidence are closely related to childhood development. A child's experience of itself is necessarily one of powerlessness and helplessness. It is part of its healthy development to forge an effective self-awareness and reach a condition of trust, and thus supplant the fear induced in it by its experience of powerlessness.

Adult experience also shows that inadequate self-respect and feelings of powerlessness are closely connected. People feel both valueless and helpless in relation to others who can do so many things so much better and so much more rapidly. People feel powerless because they do not trust themselves to meet the demands of life. But there are many types of helplessness that do not stem from inadequate self-esteem.

1. Powerlessness

Obviously in a book of this length I cannot describe and analyze all the varieties of powerlessness from which people suffer nowadays. I should like to concentrate on only three of the main areas in which feelings of powerlessness are experienced. These are feeling ineffectual with respect to myself, feeling helpless with others and their power, and powerlessness with regard to the world situation.

Feeling ineffectual

I may feel powerless about my mistakes and inadequacies. In spite of all my efforts and struggles to work on myself and change things, I keep falling back into the same old ways. I always set out with the firm intention of saying nothing about other people. But all my attempts seem doomed to fail. I constantly talk about others.

Many people suffer greatly from this fruitless effort. Whenever they go to confession or meditate they resolve firmly to spend more time on prayer. They determine to be more disciplined and to fight their basic faults, for example their sudden anger or irritability. But after a couple of weeks they realize that the effort was useless and that nothing whatsoever has changed. Nevertheless, the next time they try to change again, but with the same lack of success. The inevitable result is a feeling of powerlessness.

Some people feel powerless because they are afraid. Perhaps they have read a lot about anxiety and fear, or have even gone so far as to undergo a course of therapy and to discuss and work through their anxiety. Yet they still feel helpless as soon as anxiety symptoms seize them again. All their carefully acquired knowledge and therapeutic conversations seem useless. They are simply paralyzed by fear. Often their religious faith doesn't seem to help them either. They know that they are in God's hand, but as soon as they board an aeroplane or have to face surgery, pious words and sentiments are of no help. Faith is apparently ineffectual against this often irrational fear. Fear grips them like a savage animal. Neither head nor heart can defend them from this insidious and relentless foe.

Other people feel powerless about their emotions. They would like to overcome their envy and jealousy. But they can't stop themselves. This man feels jealous again as soon as he sees his wife talking animatedly with another man, or if his friend spends more time with other people. Then it doesn't matter how much the wife and friend insist that he is the only person they really love or like. Jealousy returns as soon as a similar situation occurs.

Others feel powerless about their impulses, whether they long for sex or food. However much they try to assert their will-power, their desires remain as strong as ever. They are constantly dominated by their basic drives. However often they try to deal with their eating problems, they fail every time. The result is a feeling of powerlessness and resignation.

One woman complained to me that she was the helpless victim of her depression. Therapy hadn't helped at all. As soon as someone criticized her, she dropped down into that deep, black hole. And as soon as she was in the hole, none of the understanding of depression she had arrived at during therapy was any use to her. Neither words nor exercises could get her out of it. She knew that when she was depressed, it should help to telephone someone, or to move around physically, go for a walk, cycle, or do some meaningful work. But none of that actually helped her in the least when she up against it. All the sensible, reasonable ideas disappeared like so much dust. She just felt quite powerless. She was the helpless victim of her depression, which seemed like some alien force with ultimate power over her. That is often the way with depression. It seems to strike suddenly, for no ascertainable reason. None of the preventative measures you are told to take works. This is another major reason for feeling powerless.

People who are psychologically disadvantaged or distressed ("mentally ill," as they used to say) often feel powerless about their problem. One woman I know suffers from what is known as "ablutomania," or a compulsive desire to wash. To date no therapy has been able to free her from this compulsion. As soon as she sits on an upholstered chair or sofa, she feels soiled and has to wash herself.

But this isn't just a problem that afflicts people who are sick or permanently disadvantaged. We all suffer from compulsions of some kind. We all feel we are victims in some way. You may feel compelled to look around outside one more time every night, just to make sure all the doors and gates are locked. You may have to reassure yourself constantly that everything on your desk is in exactly the right place. You may react angrily whenever you are criticized. Yet you seem programmed to respond in that way. When the conversation turns to certain topics, you always think you are the target of the remarks. When your old wound is touched, you cry out. There are many psychological circumstances that make us feel powerless. Many people suffer because they believe they will never be able to deal with their wounds, and that life will go on hurting them for ever.

Many people feel powerless because of something that happened when they were children. Children are powerless when their parents argue in front of them. Whatever they do to avoid a row, it seems to happen anyway. Children feel helpless when they are beaten. A child is powerless against an adult's often brutal violence. It can't fight back. The result is often ineffectual rage, and having to close up and defend oneself against pain of any kind, just to survive. When a child is treated unjustly, it may protest, but the protest is usually pointless. It is helplessly exposed to injustice. When a child is rejected, even though it does everything to make its mother like it, it feels powerless. As children we have no chance of standing up to our parents and asserting our needs. Then, as adults, we often feel similarly powerless on meeting someone who reminds us of our almighty parents or teachers. The same thing can happen when we feel inferior, or are treated unjustly.

I counselled one woman who, as a child, had to watch her mother's repeated scenes of jealous rage at her beloved father, whom her mother criticized and insulted quite vilely. The same mother would attack her too, and call her a "little whore." She always felt powerless to do anything about her mother's behaviour. She had no opportunity to discover her own worth and dignity. Later, when she came across women who resembled her mother, she felt numb or paralyzed. All the psychological awareness she had acquired in the meantime was useless when these feelings of powerlessness came over her.

Above all when we are really lonely, childhood experiences of powerlessness come to the surface again. We feel that we have to rely entirely on our own resources and that no one really understands us. No one can get to the bottom of our emotions. No one knows what we really want. Whenever these feelings of helplessness about our experiences now are out of all proportion to the actual events, we should try to remember our childhood. We should ask ourselves whether something happened to us then that made us feel the same way. Of course remembering by itself won't liberate us from this conviction of powerlessness, but the process can help us to confront it, and thus master it. At least we shall understand our feelings better. We shall no longer simply write ourselves off when we begin to feel helpless.

Trying to understand our powerlessness and talking about it may not get rid of it but it can change its effect on us. If we know where these feelings come from, they will lose their power over us, and we shall be able to deal with them more effectively.

Helpless with others

We can also feel powerless about other people. These feelings, too, may stem from childhood experience.

A woman may feel powerless with regard to her mother. She can't stand up to her. When her mother criticizes her and punches her verbally where she feels most sensitive, she crumples up and goes numb. All the discussions she has had with others about this mother-daughter situation, and all the strategies she has developed to demarcate herself from her mother, seem useless as soon as they are together. Her mother knows exactly how to wound her daughter. All she has to say is that she never has a chance of finding a husband the way she is, and immediately she has power over her. Wriggle how she may, the daughter finds she can't escape this mesmerizing force.

A man may feel powerless about his father. The father can do everything. He is intelligent and constantly devalues whatever his son does. No matter what effort the son makes, he can never stand up alongside his father. He can never satisfy his expectations. Above all, he has no means of defending himself from his father's stinging remarks and critical judgements.

Another man finds he can't assert himself in the presence of his boss. When the departmental head starts to attack him, he gives in immediately and subserviently does whatever the boss wants. He constantly thinks of telling this overbearing fellow that he is well aware of his limitations but also of his undoubted abilities; that he can do this very well, that not so well; and that surely it's sensible to recognize this; and so on. But he always gives in, and says nothing as soon as the next unjustified onslaught starts.

We may also feel powerless about people who are not authority-figures in any way, but on exactly the same level. A student may be powerless because her room-mate keeps telling her she doesn't study enough, and this gives her a permanent guilty conscience. Working on another person's guilt feelings is a well-known and subtle form of exercising power over them. There's hardly any defence against it. After all, none of us is without guilt. We are all human and used to heaping guilt on our own shoulders. If someone else awakens my natural guilt-feelings as soon as I try to do what I want, I come apart. No matter how intelligent I am and keep telling myself this is ridiculous, and that what I'm doing or not doing is perfectly acceptable, once this horrid, nagging guilt is aroused in me I can't get rid of it. It's like a poison that this so-called friend knows how to inject into me. I can't defend myself.

Parents are especially adept at making us feel guilty. When a sick mother says: "I shall just die, I know, if you don't look after me. I'm so lonely. No one cares about me. Is this all the thanks I get after everything I've done for you?" her daughter can scarcely resist the awful sensation of guilt. The remarks are calculated to hit home immediately. If her mother did die, she would never stop feeling guilty about not doing enough for her while she was alive. Whenever she goes to see her, repressed aggression wells up inside her, even though she's on her way to help her mother. To the existing burden she adds half-repressed anger with herself for letting herself be ruled by irrational guilt. She knows it will hit her as soon as she arrives and hears the inevitable complaint.

Then there are people who are unlucky in love. I'm thinking here of those who love their partner and yet are caught up in a never-ending tangle of accusations, insults, criticisms, and outbreaks of anger. They dearly want to have a good relationship with this person they love so desperately, yet life with him or her is unbearable and grows worse day by day. It doesn't matter what they do. They feel helplessly entrapped in this rotten relationship. But they can't free themselves from the deep emotion, the real love they feel for the other person. They feel dependent on the object of their love. They give him or her power over them yet remain powerless themselves to shape the relationship the way they want. Marriage counsellors are often faced with this problem: the partners' inability to communicate properly with each other and to solve their conflicts creatively. This is true even when both husband and wife are well-intentioned and genuinely want to make things work. They are still incapable of talking to one another effectively. The truth is that they are both powerless about their own feelings as individuals in the first place. As a result, they are both overwhelmingly, helplessly exposed to the wounds their partner seems determined to inflict on them.

The state of the world

When we talk about powerlessness nowadays, we very often mean how we feel about the world in general. Many people feel helpless about an anonymous bureaucracy. In spite of all the efforts of modern politicians to create a humane form of officialdom, we all know cases where the authorities are unreasonable and behave harshly to those who most need help. Many people feel powerless, for example, when officials make intolerably harsh decisions, and send people seeking political asylum back to their own countries, even though everyone knows they will certainly be persecuted or tortured once they arrive. All attempts to persuade the authorities to change their mind come up against the impenetrable wall of the law. It seems that officials are hiding behind legal justifications while their hearts turn to stone. In some countries churches provide a form of temporary asylum in these cases, and many people have found it liberating in more ways than one when their church can still offer a space where sympathizers too can counter the feeling of total helplessness.

Many people also feel powerless when they see television pictures of suffering in Ruanda or Bosnia, or the most recent location of senseless destructive conflict in Africa, the Balkans or elsewhere, especially where some kind of so-called "ethnic cleansing" is going on. They try to express their helplessness by turning to politicians. But with no effect. Some people try to get rid of the burden by donating money or clothes. But the feeling of powerlessness doesn't go away: the realization that insanely grotesque and cruel things are happening now, this minute, very close to us; things we had never dreamed were possible. We feel helpless in the face of forms of inhumanity we fondly believed were banished from the world for ever. There, on the television set in the same room, only a few feet or even inches away, we can see the poverty, screaming children, desperate mothers, raped women, maimed soldiers, corpses with torn limbs and gaping wounds, the heaps of bodies, and mass graves. And we can't do anything about it. This is a numbing, paralyzing experience. We feel profoundly helpless. Often enough, however, the result is resignation or deep depression. Of course we pray for it to stop, but God also seems to have nothing to say. In spite of all our prayer services, they are still killing refugees somewhere in the Balkans, and crowds of people are fleeing, starving, dying somewhere in Africa. And if not there, you can be sure the same or worse is happening elsewhere.

Politicians who try to do something about the Third World soon find out that they can't help people there in any really effective way. For example, missionaries who have lived in Tanzania for decades have less idea than ever before how to improve conditions and do anything for people in the long run. They feel powerless about the paralyzing structures in the country they're in, but also about the stranglehold of international economic forces. They are helpless to affect the ever-growing burden of debt and the hopeless struggle of poor countries to obtain their fair share of the big cake of global profits. Whatever they do, however hard ordinary people work, their slice constantly dwindles. Even if, after years of tactical manoeuvring, they manage to build some kind of national economy that actually works, tribal feuding eventually rips it apart. Any struggle for peaceful development and economic progress in Africa seems useless. Some politicians, indeed, have finally decided to write off Africa altogether as a dying continent. It is painful to listen to them calmly cite quite specious reasons for their lack of action, when they are really trying to cover up their powerlessness to change things.

Psychologists and religious commentators often analyze world conditions. They see the destructive effect of television on the psyche of a growing number of children, how computer games numb the emotions, and how a lack of privacy favours increasing violence in our society. The tendencies they discover in our present-day world are truly frightening. But they feel powerless to change them in any way. No one listens to what they say. No one seems to notice the dangers of so many trends. So the warning voices fade away. The very conviction that we are unable to halt the increasing drive towards a kill-crazy society, or the growing hatred of foreigners, outsiders, and people who are different, has a paralyzing effect. They stop trying. It's pointless. No one wants to know. People would rather listen to smooth-voiced phoney prophets who lull them into indifference or false security.

Nurses in clinics and centres for drop-outs at the end of their tether, for the impoverished and absolutely helpless aged, and so on, have to look after an ever-growing number of patients whose lives are artificially prolonged by feeding them with a drip and by other techniques. The nurses sense that the real point of life can't be vegetating like that. But care becomes all the more intensive. Yet whatever the nurses do to help can't change things essentially. The doctors have the final word. When they order a drip—often against the relations' will—the patient frequently has to be fed artificially at home. The nurses feel powerless against the doctors whose technical measures seem to be causing the families increased suffering and make the nurses' work all the more difficult and unsatisfactory. No appeal to basic common sense seems to have any effect. And this is only one of a multitude of situations where people feel helpless to stop some development which everyone can see is either pointless or produces results opposite to the declared intention.

In all the churches, priests and ministers have to work harder and harder to motivate their parishioners and to build up anything approaching a living community. But their efforts are fruitless. Fewer people than ever attend their talks, discussion groups and services. The numbers are constantly dropping. Some pastors and counsellors all but give up. It's like trying to stop the coast crumbling into the sea. Whatever they do, a landslide seems to be ahead. They feel powerless against the mood of the times, helpless to do anything about this creeping dechristianization of the world. Many parents who try to bring their children up as Christians have the same experience. They can't win against the dominant tendency of our age. They must helplessly watch their children forsaking the churches and looking for satisfaction elsewhere.

2. The results of powerlessness

No one experiences powerlessness without some kind of reaction. People try to escape this burden of negativity in different ways.

Anger and aggression

One response is anger. When people feel helpless about someone, a blind rage often wells up in them. They would really like to punch the cause of their powerlessness, to knock him or her down and out. John Bradshaw tells us about a man named Dawson who became like that whenever he felt as helpless as he had been as a child, when his father used to hit him. One night, when Dawson was a chucker-out in a bar, he broke a difficult customer's jaw. In situations like that he had to overcome his own fear of being beaten, and identified with his father. If something reminded him of the brutal scenes of his childhood, the old feelings of helplessness and fear would come over him. All of a sudden Dawson was transformed. Now he actually was his violent father, and socked it to people just as his father had to him.[17]

There are certainly many causes of the phenomenon of increasing violence in society, violence in schools, violence against foreigners, and so on. One reason is education. If too little notice is taken of children, they have to make an impact of some kind to ensure a reaction. If violence is used on children and they are struck or made to look ridiculous, they will resort to force themselves. Injured children hand the injuries on to others. If we don't work through the wounds of our childhood, we are condemned to wound other people in one way or another. Some children have so little self-esteem that they only feel they exist when they are violent.

Another reason for violence is certainly powerlessness to change anything in our society. Violence inevitably increases when children have little chance of a good education and of finding work later, when they have no inkling of any meaning to things, and when scarcely any notice is taken of them. Then the force they use is an expression of their own weakness, and of their feeling that they are insignificant and worthless. They use violence in an attempt to be heard.

Very often young people have never learnt how to defend themselves verbally. They don't know how to use words effectively, so they resort to violence—their only weapon. Others haven't even the words to use in the first place. In their need for attention they hit out blindly at anything and anyone around them, using the only form of utterance they have. If you are in control of yourself, you don't need to use force to make yourself noticeable. But if you have no power within or over yourself, you have to exert power somehow, above all in the form of outward violence. You have to humiliate someone in order to build up a belief in your own importance and strength. Using force on others makes you feel powerful. It's a good feeling if you're no one worth mentioning.

Violence and brutality

When people feel helpless about their own faults and weaknesses, they often react violently. They are very, very angry with themselves and try to punish themselves brutally. People who are convinced they can't do anything about their impulses often carry on a cruel campaign against their very own selves.

Someone will try to take firm control of his sexual demands. But to no effect. Naturally he keeps asserting himself. Firmness becomes harshness. To no avail. So he becomes an unmerciful judge and starts sentencing himself with increasing severity because of his sexual fantasies. More than that, he also grows into an unbending moralist ready to condemn anyone who expresses his or her sexuality. Furrer, a Swiss therapist, believes that repressed sexual desire often leads to brutality. It is certainly often apparent in moralists who use the commandments quite brutally to hammer away at everyone who offends against them and constantly issue harsh judgements on all and sundry. Such people are always on the lookout for offences. They are always spying on other people, watching for evidence of their sexual behaviour. The least evidence spurs them on to condemn and persecute their victims. In the USA this kind of puritanism leads to an extraordinary surveillance of public figures for signs of behaviour deemed sexually improper.

Nowadays, admittedly, people's sexual behaviour can be very violent. Most psychic injuries are connected with sex in some way. It is appalling to learn (in spite of all the unjust accusations of the "repressed memory syndrome" period, when irresponsible therapists induced women to "recall" non-existent suffering), how many women have certainly been sexually abused as children by men who couldn't come to terms with their own sexuality, repressed it, and then expressed it—"took it out"—on children who couldn't stand up to them.

There has been and is a vast amount of sexual abuse of minors, but of course there is also the still current phenomenon of the "abuse of abuse," when innocent men are accused of sexual misbehaviour. You can never completely defend yourself against this kind of reproach. It is another form of powerlessness. Sexual abuse and lies about imagined sexual abuse are both expressions of people's powerlessness with regard to their own and others' sexuality.

Unyielding rigour

Feeling powerless always leads to rigorism. This applies both to fundamentalist Muslims and to over-ascetic Christians who are enraged by their own inclinations. The fundamentalists of Islam feel powerless to resist the influence of western civilization. Accordingly they use proscription and violence in an attempt to block it. The same thing happens with some fundamentalist Christians. They feel powerless to fulfil their ideal of Christianity in a totally undisturbed and uniform setting. Therefore they conceal their helplessness behind fierce campaigning against all the supposed and actual immorality of their society.

The Protestant churches contain several ultra-evangelical groups whose members unmercifully criticize and even persecute their fellow-Christians and monitor their behaviour for the least deviation from the Bible and from moral codes as interpreted by these self-appointed guardians of rectitude. The Catholic churches of various countries have similar bodies, such as the militant Mariologists who are outraged by and criticize anyone who dares to talk or write about Mary in accordance with scripture rather than with these extremists' somewhat dubious interpretations of tradition. Such extremists do not hesitate to attack church authorities. In Germany, for example, Cardinal Döpfner, at heart an extremely conservative man, pursued a sensible and conciliatory policy of integrating progressive movements in the Church. He had an unshakable devotion to Our Lady. Yet he received a flood of foul-minded letters because he allowed the musical *Ave Eva* by Wilhelm Willms and Peter Janssens (a leading and scarcely outrageous contemporary musician, and a sincere Christian) to be performed in St Boniface's Abbey in Munich. Even undoubtedly pious people like Cardinal Döpfner, president of the German Bishops' Conference, are vilely insulted when they do or permit something that doesn't accord with fundamentalist prejudices.

It is difficult to talk to militant Christians. Of course they mean well. They think that they are standing up for the gospel of Jesus Christ and the pure word of God. But they can't see how unchristian their methods are. They think nothing of criticizing their "opponents" in gross and even obscene terms, and of plaguing them with sick telephone calls in the middle of the night. Why do these unmerciful Christians reject any attempt to discuss the issues that worry them? Evidently they are deeply afraid and insecure. They are worried that people might remind them of their personal inability to order and experience life as they want it to be. Of course they try to lead Christian lives. They make every effort to obey the commandments as they interpret them. But they cannot bear their inability to achieve their aims.

The history of the Church shows us that its most unrelenting moralists never actually experienced the arrival of the state of things they preached so earnestly and wanted everyone to secure as the universal divine order. Their preaching was clearly an attempt to evade their own powerlessness by vehemently demanding obedience to God's ordinances. They were afraid of their own shadows, of the immorality of their own hearts, and they sought to escape their own intolerable anxiety by attacking others as outrageously immoral. Because they feared the devils that possessed their own hearts they demonized other people. But their powerlessness led them to exercise a ruthless and brutal power over those to whom they preached their inhuman morality. Their fear of their own shadow selves forced them to make others afraid of guilt and sin.

Self-punishment

People who express their powerlessness in anger and violence often direct them not only against others but against themselves. If you feel helpless to realize your own ideals, as often as not you are inclined to be unyieldingly rigorous with yourself. You try to deny your impulses and emotions. You deny yourself any possibility of joy and pleasure. You punish yourself incessantly if you have offended against some commandment or rule.

Self-punishment (what psychiatrists call "intrapunitive behaviour") can even take the form of an accident or a sickness, or of unbelievably masochistic practices used to punish oneself for every little failure. Cruelty is often internalized in a twisted conscience. Then the moral guardian inside you becomes an unrelenting judge of your own mistakes. People like this are constantly engaged in an inward police action. They drag themselves before the judgement-seat of their unmerciful super-ego. They may believe in divine mercy, but they are quite unjust with themselves. They sentence themselves for the least peccadillo and carry on a mental terror campaign against their supposedly inadequate selves.

One scarcely unrepresentative woman I know eats too much. That seems to be her nature. She just can't stop. Her whole life is built round eating and starving herself. She thinks and talks about nothing else. Fasting rather than starving is a well-proven method of achieving inner freedom. But if I fast to punish myself for my excessive appetite, I am merely treating myself harshly and cruelly.

Then fasting will not liberate me but only make me aggressive and dissatisfied.

Resignation and despair

Another reaction to the experience of your own helplessness is just giving in. And resignation is really a form of despair.

You have tried again and again to overcome your inadequacies but you keep failing. Constant disappointment with your own efforts leads to resignation. You stop trying and simply live as it comes, without any major aims or goals. Your ideals collapse. It's all pointless. You can't do any more about it all. Outwardly you go on working industriously. You may even be very successful. But your basic theme tune is a form of despair. You work all the harder to get rid of the uneasy feeling that despair and emptiness are ruling you. But there they are again as soon as you stop work and have nothing to do.

Resignation and despair are often the background to people's wholehearted devotion to work or pleasure. They stare out at us from the smiling faces in advertisements. We encounter them in the behaviour of people who run games-shows on television, or of fun-organizers at holiday camps. We see them in the faces of managers who work round the clock to escape their inner vacuum. Their victims are people who have given up looking for anything, or really striving to achieve something worthwhile. They are resigned to a world of tedious and tawdry pseudo-achievement, yet they often still sense somewhere within them a voice that says there is something else that's better than this, and that God wants us to be more than superficial.

We also find resignation and despair in social and political life. Politicians and economists stop fighting to improve the environment or campaigning for more justice in the world, because they see no chance of success. They know that we are sitting on a powder-keg, but they shut their eyes to the dismal truth (with which they are better acquainted than anyone else), and "just carry on with their job" or tell themselves: "It's just a holding operation, after all."

Some politicians and managers who were committed in the past have to cover up a truly desperate emptiness by permanent, even furious activity. They are constantly in and out of trains and aeroplanes and seemingly engaged in work for undeniably good ends. Essentially, however, they have given up the struggle. As individuals, they are no longer trying because they feel powerless to achieve anything in the world as it is.

You sometimes feel that the fine-sounding words and speeches uttered by politicians are chosen and composed merely to hide their helplessness, which they realized long ago and resigned themselves to. If you criticize politicians or economists who are obvious workaholics, they will usually be deeply offended. You can easily see that their immense workload is simply a cover for their inner powerlessness, always present as a source of profound anxiety beneath the outer rush of constant activity.

3. Dealing with powerlessness

A. *Human ways*

We can't simply discard powerlessness. It is an essential aspect of being human. But we can learn how to cope with it in various ways. Of course we can react by simply resigning ourselves to it, or by behaving aggressively. But we can also shape our lack of power creatively. If we respond to it actively it can be of benefit in our lives. It can inspire us to do whatever is within our range of possibilities, for ourselves or for the world we live in. It can become a source of imagination and creativity for reshaping this world in a more human way.

We are often able to overcome our powerlessness if we learn to make effective use of it. We shall no longer feel ineffectual if we take the initiative and do all we can. In the following pages I shall discuss some ways of responding positively to our lack of power over ourselves and the world situation.

With others

Civil action is one way of overcoming social powerlessness. People join together to fight for a common cause. If they tried to work on their own, they would be ineffectual, say when trying to preserve the peace of the area where they live. Jointly, they have a chance. Together they can force local councillors or even national politicians to rethink the situation and find other ways of diverting traffic, for instance.

Civil action is often a means of influencing political decisions that may depend on coalition pressures and are made in spite of evidence that another course is better. But many initiatives are not fighting against but for something. They might be campaigns for a crèche or for some other means of improving child care in the area, for home-helps and day nursing, or for efficient social visiting and aid, for more children's playgrounds, or just groups working to organize something as simple as street parties. Actions of this kind help to assure people that they are not inescapably subject to social pressures, but can create a form of community in the midst of this anonymous world and help to shape communal life.

Other ways out of powerlessness are attempts to improve communication. Firms, parishes, families, religious Orders and other groups and organizations often suffer from inadequate communication. But as soon as people find they cannot talk to one another effectively, nothing gets done. The company goes on operating, but it no longer shapes its future, and no longer has any influence on people; it has ceased to produce new ideas. The same is true of religious Orders and presbyteries. When people can't communicate appropriately, life dries up. Individuals may be working away quite energetically, but nothing seems to come together. And the community is no longer spreading its due share of creativity.

One way of escaping from the same old ineffectual daily grind is to try out new ways of communicating. People can start discussing their repressed or unused feelings, opportunities, possibilities, talents and abilities. They can talk about their fears, but also their dreams and expectations for the future. This will give rise to a power potential to set against the lack of effective power. If you look at the future hopefully you will find pleasure and even joy in helping to shape your community and, at the same time, a small part of the world.

On your own

A personal way of coping with powerlessness is to set about remaking yourself as far as that is sensible and possible. Traditionally, working to change yourself in the way I am thinking of is known as asceticism (or "ascesis," from *askesis*, the Greek word for training or self-discipline). This means that we shape our lives ourselves by going without, by discipline, and by bringing due order into our existence.

Asceticism really means good practice. It means training myself to a new degree of proficiency and to inner freedom. Nowadays we run the danger of continually complaining that we can't do anything about the personalities we happen to be; that we are powerless to change the selves that nurture (upbringing and education) has moulded out of what nature (our genetic inheritance) has made us. But it is possible.

Asceticism means actually enjoying shaping ourselves, taking pleasure in working on our selves, discovering something in ourselves, and shaping ourselves. If I am ascetic, I may learn to live as an independent human being and not to have my life directed by others. I shall have power over myself instead of ineffectually watching others control me or letting my emotions run my life. I shall not be the mere victim of my mistakes and foibles. I can work on myself and change something in my life. I can free myself from some of the compulsions that seem to rule me. Admittedly, when I try to be ascetic I shall find that I always come up against certain limits and experience my powerlessness in new ways. I shall discover that I can't do everything I would like to do, and that even the ascetic way of life is not a means of achieving total self-mastery. But, at the very least, I shall certainly be able to turn my particular lack of power into a way of experiencing some kind of grace in my life, and not just resign myself to it pointlessly.

If you feel helpless with regard to your fears or emotions, therapeutic counselling is often a sensible resource. In therapy you can uncover the reasons for your fear or anger and find a way of coming to terms with the traumas of the past. But it won't be enough merely to discover the causes. That alone won't heal you. Sometimes you have to relive the pains you suffered as a child. You will have to mourn over them, as it were, in order to discard the automatic reactions you have inherited from your childhood. Then you can slowly learn to cope creatively with your fear or psychic wounds. You will no longer be the helpless victim of your fear but react to it appropriately. You will begin to realize that it has a meaning, and that even this same anxiety that has tortured you can help you to find the right way ahead in your life.

Therapy can't help you to reach a state in which you never feel powerless or ineffectual again. But it can help you to deal with your helplessness. It can show you a way to become reconciled to it, and then to try out the opportunities that your nature and your circumstances offer you of moving ahead effectively. Jung says that it is a matter of realizing that there is a certain point in your life at which you yourself just have to take the full responsibility for it. You have to say Yes to your past and to treat it as the material you are offered for shaping your future. When you become responsible for your own life you will find you are dealing actively with your powerlessness. You will see that you can't do everything you want. But you will also begin to understand that you really can change some things in your life. When you are convinced of that, you will no longer be determined or controlled by your psychic injuries and difficulties. Instead they will become a source of new opportunities and possibilities.

An enormous number of people nowadays stay stuck in the ruts or mud of complaining about their own bad luck. They continually tell other people what an awful childhood they had. They moan about how unfortunate they have always been. But they never try to find ways of healing their psychic wounds. Above all, they fail because they do not look for the opportunities and new ways ahead that are certainly there: somewhere in their very own selves.

Useful rituals

Many people today think they are ruled by objective forces and compulsions. They feel powerless to do anything about them. There are some effective rites and rituals that can help us to give our lives a certain healing shape and order.

If I develop a set of rituals, for beginning or closing the day, for instance, an order for shaping my weekend, perhaps, I may begin to feel that I am living myself instead of being lived by others and other forces. If I impose my own order on my life, in however small a way, I shall have the actual experience that I am not helplessly exposed to a world of indifferent or malign controlling powers. I can give my own life an order that I actually enjoy.

Freud tells us that the main function of rituals is to banish fear. Lack of order and form produces fear, and rituals help us to overcome that fear. Rituals are part of any healthy culture and way of life. Our own private culture, the order we decide to give our own lives, liberates us from the feeling that other people are running us. We can feel in charge of ourselves for the first time. Rituals reinforce our feeling of having an identity and give us an assurance that we are free to decide something for ourselves.

It is always pleasurable to shape our lives in decent, healthy, and even beautiful ways. Rituals can be the first steps in giving our lives a form of order and dignity that deserves to be termed beautiful. They can express our imagination and our sense of personal freedom, for, after all, we devise them for ourselves alone. They can encourage a very real conviction that we are not helpless as far as controlling life is concerned but are responsible for ourselves and can do something to re-order our way of life beneficially.

Freeing yourself from others' power

Many people feel powerless with respect to others. They find they have no means of defence against their boss, marriage partner, colleagues at work, and so on, who seem constantly to want to irritate and hurt them. They feel helplessly victimized by spitefulness and meanness. Then rage, a justifiable explosion, can be a major form of healing, and can actually help us to free ourselves from this particular kind of powerlessness.

Fury, or losing our temper, can give us the strength to distance ourselves from the people who have injured us, and, as it were, to eject the enemy who has so wounded us from the place they have come to occupy in our consciousness. A reliable principle for dealing with people who hurt and control the way you think about yourself is to remember that others only have the power over you that you let them have. I can hardly stop myself reacting sensitively when someone is vile to me. But I decide whether I spend the whole day afterwards going over it again and again, carrying on an endless conversation with myself about how hurt I feel. I can't suppress every feeling of anger that wells up in me. But it is in my power to decide whether I go on wallowing in that anger, or distance myself from it.

Anger is actually a wholly positive force. It drives me to change something. I can alter a situation that I feel angry about by organizing things differently. Or I can change my relationship with the person who makes me angry. Then anger is the power I have to distance myself from that person, to eject him or her from me inwardly, and to put up a "Trespassers Will Be Prosecuted!" notice for him or her at the entry to my inner self. I forbid myself to think about the other person in my house or in my room. He or she just can't get in. I don't allow him or her the pleasure of ruining my dinner-time for me. It is up to me whether I feel helpless in front of that person, or free myself from his or her power by distancing myself and ejecting him or her from my heart.

I often counsel women who were sexually abused as children. The worst thing is that they are not only angry about it but feel guilty that they did not defend themselves, or that they somehow submitted to the same experience again and again. I try to give these women the courage to experience their anger effectively by simply ejecting the man who wounded their dignity and value. Very often this is the beginning of their healing process.

If the other person who has wounded me still has a place in my heart, forgiveness would only be masochism. I would only be scratching at the old wound. I have to throw the culprit right out of my life to see him or her objectively and forgive him or her effectively. Then forgiveness will be what it should be: final liberation from another person's power over me.

If you can't forgive by giving up then you will remain under the control of the person who injured you. You will bear the same old injury with you wherever you go. You have to forgive and eject. Some people just cannot heal themselves because they cannot forgive and forget in this sense.

Dealing with power

Power is the opposite of powerlessness. Nowadays we have a twofold relationship to power. Power makes us think immediately of the misuse of power and of the power that we exercise over others.

Power sounds negative. But it is entirely positive. Power is the ability to do something freely and of our own strength and will.[18] Accordingly, power is power over myself: the capability of shaping myself, and of living my own life instead of having it lived for me.

The Greek and Latin words for power, *dynamis* and *potestas*, come from roots meaning ability and capability. But *dynamis* also means force and strength. The writer of the Gospel according to Luke sees Jesus as possessing unusual strength. When he is conceived, it is by "the power of the most high" (Luke 1:35). Jesus works his miracles (= *dynameis* = deeds of strength or power) through the power and strength of God. The disciples share in Christ's strength and power. They also work miracles by his power. For the Greeks, power was identical with being, and an essential attribute of God. The Christian who shares in the nature of God ("It is through him that God's greatest and most precious promises have become available to us," 2 Pet. 1:3ff), also shares in the power of God. He or she is summoned to shape his or her own life and the world according to God's will.

Power is only secondarily a commission to lead and direct. When I am with people who are responsible for supervising and leading others, they often complain that they can't do anything with their difficult colleagues or employees, and that frequently they have to resign themselves helplessly to this experience.

In fact, real leadership is a response to the experience of powerlessness. Leading means discovering new possibilities and releasing them in people. Jesus himself shows us how we should understand power in a positive sense: "Among the heathen it is their kings who lord it over them, and their rulers are given the title of 'benefactors.' But it must not be so with you! Your greatest man must become like a junior and your leader must be a servant" (Luke 22:25ff). Absolute monarchs and dictators rule nations by dominating them and deciding exactly what they should and should not do. They exert power over their countries by humiliating other people. They keep people small in order to appear big themselves. They live at the expense of the oppressed.

Yet the powerful always call themselves benefactors of humankind. They use their power to look good in front of others. They use power for their own purposes and thus abuse it. But the power exercised by leaders in the sense approved by Jesus is a form of service. It is of help to people and to life. It releases people's abilities and possibilities. It puts them in touch with their own dreams, aspirations and potential.

Each of us is always leader and led at one and the same time. Each of us has already received power together with his or her life. Power is the longing to shape life and the joy of doing so. It is also the desire to arouse life in people and the pleasure of doing so. It is in this sense that we share in the power of God.

In Christian circles we often experience a twofold relation to power. We are reluctant or refuse to exercise it because it doesn't seem to fit our ideal of selflessness and love of our neighbours. But the sad thing is that repressed power is often worse for people than naked power. You can defend yourself against the open exercise of power, whereas you are powerless against power that is exercised subtly and in hidden ways from a basis of repression.

Precisely because power is notionally proscribed in the Church, its actual exercise often takes a destructive form. A power behind which the person exercising it has taken care to conceal his or her part in it is destructive, not constructive. A major task for the churches would be an attempt to rethink the practice of power.

Power is also the longing to shape something, the joy of sharing in the creative moulding of this world, of liberating life in people, and of serving life, so that the life that God has given us can bear fruit in as many people as possible. Power, says Karl Rahner, is "a gift of God, the expression of his own power, and an aspect of God's representation in this world."[19]

Klaus Hemmerle, a former Bishop of Aachen, Germany, wrote that the real purpose of power is "the powerfulness of what is good and right, in the form of the common good. Power is therefore a harmony of the will with the world, 'horizontally,' in harmony with other wills in a society deciding and shaping a common world, and 'vertically', in harmony with the norm of the good and rightful. In short, power is the effective ordering of human society as existence in the world."[20] Instead of standing there helplessly in face of our personal difficulties and the problems of the world, we should be thankful for the power that God has given us, and use it to order our own lives and the world according to the will of God.

B. *Religious ways*

Religious education has often been responsible for people feeling helpless. If God is presented one-sidedly as an omnipotent Ruler, people are often forced to see themselves as small and powerless. What chance do I have of escaping this strict and punitive God who can see everything? Whenever I make a mistake, he can find out—in fact, he has already caught me at it in advance. I am a helpless victim of his omnipotence, so it seems. Sometimes what religious people and teachers tell us amounts to affirming that we are "naturally" depraved and corrupt, or they even say so straightforwardly. Of course that makes us feel all the more helpless and useless, because it means we are condemned to be sinners. For the rest of our lives we shall be striking our breasts before God and asking him to forgive us.

Some teachers and priests seem to forget about Jesus' humanity completely and merely stress his divinity. They play up his miracles to such an extent that we feel even smaller, incapable, and incompetent as a result. Much religious talk, preaching, and education lays such stress on the divinity of Jesus and the omnipotence of God that, far from helping us in our lack of power and with our feelings of inadequacy, it simply reinforces them.

But Jesus showed us people in another light. He saw them quite differently. When he met people who were crushed by the sheer awfulness of life, whom others had reduced to the level of nonentities and had constantly belittled, and who were left weak or spineless or washed out, he tried his best to lift them up again and show each of them their undeniable dignity and worth in the sight of God.

In his resurrection, Christ raised us all up in that way, supported us, and told us exactly the same thing. That was why the early Christians always prayed standing up.

They did so in memory of Jesus' resurrection and to show they were unique individuals of full value before God. Their prayer was a constant reminder and experience of the fact that Jesus had made them fully aware of their dignity and worth as human beings in the sight of God.

Humans are empowered

The author of the Gospel according to John portrays Jesus, even in the humiliation of his passion, as someone endowed with royal dignity. He portrays him as a king to show us that we can preserve our own God-given dignity even in the harshest and most degrading circumstances of our lives. When Pilate asks Jesus: "What have you done anyway?," he replies: "My kingdom is not founded in this world—if it were, my servants would have fought to prevent my being handed over. . . . But in fact my kingdom is not founded on all this!" (John 18:36). Because Jesus' kingdom is not established in this world, neither Pilate nor the soldiers who hold him captive, torture, mock, and crucify him have any power over him. Outwardly, to be sure, Jesus undergoes a vile death on the cross. For the author of the Gospel, however, Jesus' crucifixion is actually the coronation of the real King.

What we read about Jesus here applies to all of us too. In the depth of our sufferings, whenever we are rejected, criticized, made fools of, despised, hurt, and traumatized we can say: "My kingdom is not founded in this world." We have a divine value in us that no worldly power can take away from us because it is not founded in this world. Even in the ultimate helplessness of death, no one and nothing can take that royal dignity and empowerment away from us.

On the last Sunday in the church year the Catholic Church celebrates the feast of Christ the King. The point made on other occasions (such as Epiphany)—that is, that Christ is King of the whole world—has to be re-emphasized at the end of the liturgical year. It is not just a matter of proclaiming Christ as King, but of showing us that in him and with him we too can sense and experience our royal dignity and value.

It is important to remember that "King" here stands for someone who is in control of himself or herself, who is fully aware of and able to govern his or her passions and longings, and is not helplessly exposed and delivered up to his or her enemies. For the Greeks, a king was a wise, competent and judicious person who knew all the heights and depths of human existence. Martin Buber reminds us of a saying of Rabbi Shlomo: "What is the worse thing that evil can make us do?—To make people forget that they are the sons and daughters of kings."[20]

We celebrate the feast of Christ the King so that we can behave more confidently in our everyday life. We can do so because we know we are empowered. We are truly royal persons with the dignity and value due to the fully acknowledged children of God. If we understand the liturgy properly, we shall see that it doesn't constantly stress our inadequacy, but insists that we should discover our true nature as Christians. It asks us constantly to realize that we have a right to share in Christ's kingdom. It tells us that God has given us a dignity and value that allow us to hold our heads high whatever the circumstances, because ultimately no force or authority in this world has power over us. We are free human beings because nothing in this world can control the divine core within us. Nothing can reach and manipulate the very centre of our being where God dwells inside us.

Freeing yourself from the world's power

Mystics, too, refer to this divine core when they tell us that we have a quiet space inside us where only God dwells and where this world is powerless. The God who lives within us is the God of Exodus, the God who delivers us from overseers who force us to work beyond our capacities, who make us surrender our freedom only so that we can taste the fleshpots of Egypt.

God liberates us from the power of the world, from the power of human beings, their claims and expectations, their judgements and prejudices. And he frees us from the power of our own super-ego, from self-accusation and self-reproach, from self-punishment and self-devaluation.

The theology of baptism tells us that we died to this world together with Christ when we were baptized. In this context, dying to the world has no negative implications but means taking the way of freedom. If I am dead to this world, it has no power over me. In baptism I learn that there is another life in me: a divine life to which this world cannot gain access. Every celebration of the Eucharist is intended to remind us of the reality of our baptism, so that we celebrate not only death and resurrection but our death to this world. When we take holy water on entering a church (or, in some places, on leaving a house), we constantly remind ourselves that we draw life from another reality, and one over which this world fortunately has no power.

Coming to terms with your own lack of power

It is an age-old human temptation to call on God's supreme power to redress our own lack of power, and to imagine that prayer and a pious life will free us from our helplessness. But the paradox of Christianity is that we have to come to terms with our powerlessness. God revealed himself in his powerlessness in Jesus Christ.

For Dietrich Bonhoeffer, a German patriot and heroic Christian who was executed by the Nazis during World War II for his steadfast opposition to evil, the experience of God's powerlessness was an absolutely decisive event. It led him to rethink his theology as he waited for death in Tegel prison: "Before God and with him we live without God. God allows himself to be edged out of the world and on to the cross. God is weak and powerless in the world, and that is exactly the way, the only way, in which he can be with us and help us."[21]

The image of a powerless God implies something quite different from the image of the omnipotent Ruler. When God reveals himself as powerless in the incarnation and death of his Son, he asks us to be reconciled to our own powerlessness. But this powerlessness before God is not a state in which I feel small before God who is so great, but a powerlessness with God, in which I sense God's closeness to me. Then our powerlessness becomes the area where we experience God. At the very point where I've lost my grip, where I can't do any more, where I can't manage any longer, where I'm at the end of my tether, where I fail, God can take me up and support me. All I can do then is hold out my empty hands to God and give myself up to him.

For Christians, powerlessness is an essential part of existence. Anyone who believes in the crucified Christ sees God's powerlessness displayed in him. Jesus ends up in the powerlessness of the cross. Paul, the apostle who preached the way of the cross, had to learn by the experience of his own body that he was helpless against what he called the thorn in his flesh. This "thorn" was clearly a physical handicap or severe illness that caused Paul great difficulty in his preaching. He asked the Lord three times to free him from it. But Christ led Paul into a mystery and showed him a function of his grace that was expressed in the very weakness he found so devastating: "Three times I begged the Lord for it to leave me, but his reply has been: 'My grace is enough for you: for where there is weakness my power is shown the more completely.' Therefore, I have cheerfully made up my mind to be proud of my weaknesses, because they mean a deeper experience of the power of Christ. I can even enjoy weaknesses, suffering, privations, persecutions and difficulties for Christ's sake. For my very weakness makes me strong in him" (2 Cor. 12: 9-10).

Paul believed that he could proclaim Christ's message effectively only if he appeared to be supremely efficient, and the Corinthians thought he was in the best of health. He had to learn from Christ how to make use not only of his strength but just as much of his weakness and powerlessness. He had to discover, in fact, that he could achieve what was necessary through them.

We are open to God's grace precisely where we experience our own powerlessness. Whatever breaks us also cracks us open, as it were, to receive the love of God, for our own will no longer stands in the way of God's action.

At one time or another in the course of our lives, we all experience what Paul felt in his own body: that God's power can be experienced at the very point where we have reached zero, when we have completely lost control, and when we have to admit the painful truth that we can never guarantee anything of our own volition.

Obviously we have to keep telling ourselves that our strength comes from God and not from ourselves. We shall encounter our final helplessness in death. Then everything will be taken from us, and we shall be in charge of nothing any longer. Then all we can do is to let ourselves fall helplessly into God's loving hands. The powerlessness of death is already apparent in the powerlessness that we experience every day of our lives. Accordingly, each instance of our lack of power that we suffer now asks us to be reconciled with our mortal nature, with our frailty, and with the weakness of our physical existence. At the same time, however, powerlessness invites us to believe in the power of God; in the resurrection power in which God's strength will also be triumphantly available to us.

The experience we derive from our powerlessness is liberating. It is the experience that we do not have to do everything ourselves; that we have to be weak; and that in our weakness we are buttressed by God's own strength. If I refuse any kind of weakness, I must always live in fear of failure. But when I know that the grace of God can be apparent not only in my strength but in my weakness, then I can open my empty hands confidently and stretch them out to God. Then I shall experience a deep inner peace and freedom from any pressure or compulsion to perfect myself by my own power.

Prayer and empowerment

Prayer can liberate us from the power other people have over us. We can see this from the parable of the dishonest magistrate (Luke 18:1-8). Jesus uses the example of the widow fighting for her rights and asking for protection from the man who was trying to ruin her to illustrate the effects of prayer. The magistrate neither fears God nor respects his fellow-humans and refuses to help her. "But later he said to himself: 'Although I don't fear God and have no respect for men, yet this woman is such a nuisance that I shall give judgement in her favour, or else her constant visits will be the death of me!'"

Prayer assures us of our right to life. Prayer takes me into a realm of peace and quiet where God dwells in me, and where no one has power over me. Our enemies have no entry to this peaceful area—neither the external nor the internal foes that so upset my life and prevent me from living as I would like and ought to live. In that space a crooked judge who doesn't care about God or humanity is powerless.

The dishonest magistrate stands for our super-ego, the part of our mind that follows social rules, isn't interested in our true well-being, and couldn't care less about our God-given dignity and worth. In prayer God provides justice and maintains and enacts my rights. There he leads me into the realm of freedom where, in the innermost reaches of peace and silence, I can experience true life. I can take shelter in that protective space, and be my own true self whole and entire.

Of course prayer won't liberate me directly from the powerlessness that I feel as the victim of my worries, pains and anxieties, or in and about the world as it is. Prayer isn't a magical solution to all problems. But in prayer I can discover the quiet place in myself where the problems of the world and my own noisy thoughts have no right of entry. If someone has hurt me deeply, then the wound doesn't simply vanish when I enter the quiet space within for meditation. But I begin to see what it means in relation to other things. During that moment of prayer I feel free from the injury done me. My heart is still wounded, but the injury itself cannot enter the ground of the soul (Tauler), the cell within (Catherine of Siena), the sanctuary, the inner shrine where human beings have no right of entry.

There is a region within me where feelings of fear, rage, jealousy, and sudden anger cannot penetrate and no one can hurt me. Yet as soon as I leave the prayer enclosure inside me and return to my everyday world, I shall find that I am still sensitive to people's criticism. The wound will go on smarting and my heart will be as injured as before. But it will also realize that it is not totally affected by what I have suffered. My heart will know that deep inside it there is a space quite untouched by pain and sickness. Even in the midst of suffering we can be aware of healing and liberation, and know peace and consolation.

Sharing in Christ's power

Jesus makes a promise to the disciples who have followed him: "Believe me when I tell you that in the next world, when the Son of Man shall sit down on his glorious throne, you who have followed me will also sit on twelve thrones and become judges of the twelve tribes of Israel" (Matt. 19:28). He says that they will be allowed to share in his own power and rule. This is a question not only of the power that they will enjoy at the end of the ages, but of their activity in the world now. In fact they already share in Jesus Christ's power. "They will drive out evil spirits in my name; they will speak with new tongues; they will pick up snakes, and if they drink anything poisonous it will do them no harm; they will lay their hands upon the sick and they will recover" (Mark 16:7ff). Christ gave his disciples the same power that he had over evil spirits. The authority of Christ's word is also evident in what the disciples say when they speak in Jesus' name and in his Spirit. When the Spirit of Christ is clearly present in an individual, evil spirits just cannot stand the pressure. It forces them into the light of day and they have to leave the person they have kept prisoner for so long. Where Christ's Spirit is effectively present, unhealthy and destructive obsessions, misleading ideas, complexes, and confused, disruptive or unruly thinking no longer have any power over human beings.

The question, however, is whether and how what the Bible says about the power of Christ and his disciples can help us today, especially in our attempts to overcome our own weaknesses and ineffectiveness in the face of the present world situation. Of course it isn't sufficient merely to repeat what the Bible says about God's supreme power and the rule of Christ. A few examples may serve to show how faith in God's power can liberate people from powerlessness.

When talking to people I often feel powerless to help them. The individual I am speaking to is often so obsessed by one-sided or confused ideas, or is so marked by childhood traumas, that he or she scarcely hears a word I say. All attempts to find out together what could be of help to this person end in failure. Then I find it a real help to pray for the individual in question when I am in choir with the other monks, and I ask God to vanquish our enemies: "Save me from my persecutors, for they are too strong for me. Bring me out of prison, so that I may give thanks to your name" (Ps. 142:7). "In your steadfast love cut off my enemies, and destroy all my adversaries, for I am your servant" (Ps. 143:12). I can feel the power of God in these words from the Psalms, and I know that God's power is stronger than all the forces that bind, imprison, and isolate the person I am trying to counsel.

I use much the same words to pray when my own inadequacies make me feel totally powerless: "Save me, O Lord, from my enemies; I have fled to you for refuge" (Ps. 143:9). In situations like that, I sometimes use Psalm 31 as my prayer, remembering that when Jesus was dying on the cross he repeated the same words to his Father. Then, when he experienced the ultimate weakness of death, he sensed the power of the Father in whom he trusted: "For your name's sake lead me and guide me, take me out of the net that is hidden for me, for you are my refuge. Into your hand I commit my spirit; you have redeemed me, O Lord, faithful God!" (Ps. 31:5ff). When I pray those words I am filled with hope that, even in the direst of seemingly hopeless situations, confidence in God's help and closeness will hold me up and strengthen me, so that I do not despair but entrust myself to the hand of God.

Powerlessness in the face of the world situation is the kind of helplessness that we suffer from most of all nowadays. But we have to beware of simply citing God's omnipotence as if it were a magic amulet that will do the trick in the end, and thus make up for our own inability to do anything about world events. For it is part of the experience of faith that almighty God seems to remain silent and withdrawn, and that we see no sign of his power to affect things.

The fact that God doesn't intervene to stop the cruelties happening in Bosnia and Ruanda and in so many other places around the world is a challenge to our faith. What use is it to talk of an almighty God when he just looks on helplessly while people destroy his creation? The people of Israel always found it painful when God apparently withdrew from the scene of their sufferings and disasters without intervening in any way.

The history of Israel is a history of constant failures and powerlessness. In Europe today the Christian churches are certainly experiencing much the same thing. They feel their helplessness acutely as, notwithstanding all their prayers and all their efforts, more and more of their members drift away, and people increasingly lose interest in them. As Christians, with regard to the situation of the churches and in view of our own problems, we can pray together with the Psalmist: "Your foes have roared within your holy place; they set up their emblems there. . . . We do not see our emblems; there is no longer any prophet, and there is no one among us who knows how long. How long, O God, is the foe to scoff? Is the enemy to revile your name forever? Why do you hold back your hand; why do you keep your hand in your bosom?" (Ps. 74:4, 8-11). Or our experience is like Isaiah's: "We wait for light, and lo! there is darkness; and for brightness, but we walk in gloom. We grope like the blind along a wall, groping like those who have no eyes; we stumble at noon as in the twilight, among the vigorous as though we were dead. . . . We wait for justice, but there is none; for salvation, but it is far from us" (Isa. 59:9-11).

For many people, God's powerlessness is a temptation to despair of him altogether and to jettison their faith for good. How can God permit all this if he is omnipotent? Trying to carry on in spite of the fact that God doesn't intervene when he evidently ought to is a challenge to every Christian's faith, and only bearable in view of Christ's suffering on the cross.

When I consider the poverty and misery all over the world, and the cruelties in the Balkans and Ruanda and so many other places, which I have to watch without any possibility of doing anything about them, prayer doesn't cancel the powerlessness I feel. But it does help me to remember my assurance that in the end the murderers will not triumph over their victims and that, in spite of everything, the world remains in God's hand and not in the hands of those insane torturers, executioners, and warmongers. Your faith must be strong indeed not to despair when you realize your own helplessness. Then, of course, it is much easier to close your eyes and to play down the situation in the war zones, or to attribute all the guilt to the people on the spot. But faith in God's omnipotence is not a kind of opium that allows me to drift off into oblivion and indifference to human need and suffering. Instead, prayer for these people should also motivate me to do whatever I possibly can for them. Prayer and action, contemplation and struggle, submission and resistance (Bonhoeffer), mysticism and politics go together.

Prayer is not something I can simply withdraw to and hide in. Very often prayer asks me to do what God has already given me the potential to achieve as the person I really am. It is a way of realizing what I am "destined" to carry out. Trust in God's almighty power is not some kind of comforter that is always available to stick in our mouths when we are frustrated. Instead (to change the metaphor), it can ignite a spark of hope in the midst of the dark and senseless anger that wells up in us when we realize how hopelessly ineffectual we are. And that same spark of hope can become a light helping our rational selves to work out something meaningful and effective that will change the way we are.

The power of prayer

The monks of Mount Athos believe that the only reason why our world has not already disappeared in dust and ashes is that people continue to pray all over the world and that not a single minute passes without someone addressing God in prayer. Staretz Siluan is sure that "only prayer is sufficiently strong to affect the course of history significantly and to restrict the extent of evil."[22] The Swiss still believe that they owe their centuries-old peace to the prayers of Nicholas of Flüe.

You cannot prove the effectiveness of prayer. But all religions are convinced that prayer represents an immense potential force against the destructive powers of this world. Some members of a group belonging to the worldwide peace movement once asked me whether prayer was actually any use. Surely, they argued, demonstrations were much more likely to have some effect on the minds and inclinations of politicians. Of course I cannot prove whether and how prayer transforms the thought-processes of those who hold the reins of power in this world. Demonstrations certainly have a certain value in their own right. But I think that prayer has the real power to get things moving in the world. Think about it. What actually caused the change in Russia and the former Soviet bloc, and what actually brought about the peace between Israel and the Arabs, and the end of apartheid in South Africa? I believe in the power of prayer. I know that prayer can move mountains.

The power of love

As Christians, we believe not only in the power of prayer but just as much in the power of love. God's love shone out here on earth in Jesus Christ. It healed the sick and put people on the right path. Jesus' love pure and simple was apparent on the cross where he showed that he still loved the very people who nailed him to it.

The same love asks us to stop judging ourselves as we do. If Jesus himself still loves the people who killed him, I can certainly rest assured that he loves me, and I can surely love myself.

For the last two thousand years, all over the world, the love of Jesus Christ has established pockets of true humanity where that same love has repeatedly grasped and affected people who have made at least some part of the world more human and lovable. Love has constantly eroded and then destroyed the barriers between people and peoples.

Prayer contains a powerful impulse to love. But love has to be visible and take effect in mind, intention, and attitude as well as in action. It was love that Anwar Sadat, a pious Muslim, felt in his heart and that spurred him to make peace with Israel. It was the love in Martin Luther King that broke through the obstacles between Blacks and Whites. The reconciliation between France and Germany happened not only because of politicians, but because there were enough loving people on both sides for whom love was stronger than the hatred that had produced a century of rivalry. Fairy-stories, myths, and legends tell us how utterly love can change someone, for it can dissolve stone and even turn animals into human beings. In recent decades we have seen repeated evidence of this. Love tore down the wall between the two Germanies. And love always has the power to turn even maddened enemies, prepared to fight one another to the death, into human beings who walk together into the future.

Love is paradoxical, for its strength is apparent precisely where it is powerless. Love dispenses with all outward force. Jesus' love is evident in the powerlessness of his death. Love walks through the valley of the shadow of death fearing no evil, and utterly transforms the darkness that reigns there. Because of his love, Jesus does not take up arms against his enemies and murderers. He breaks through the fatal circle of retribution. He subverts evil with his love and dissolves it. The author of the Gospel according to John tells us what Jesus' love is like when he describes him washing his disciples' feet: "He had always loved his own who were in the world, and now he was to show the full extent of his love" (John 13:1). Jesus bends down to wash the disciples' sore and dirty feet, and dries them with a towel. Since Jesus' death on the cross, the power of this divine love has enabled countless Christians to commit themselves to the world's problems and to re-shaping it. Their powerless love has been the strongest power in this world. There can be no doubt of that. It has had the most enduring effect on our earth.

In the area of personal relationships, I am sure, we have all known occasions when someone's disinterested love has changed things utterly. There is the old Hasidic (Jewish) story, for instance, of a father who couldn't do anything with his wayward son, so he took him to see the rabbi. The man of God embraced the boy and held him tight in his arms. A day later he returned him to his father, completely changed. Or there was the five-year-old girl who had been sexually abused by her father but who came to new life in her infant school under the loving care of a new teacher, a nun who took over the class one day. I remember that woman's particularly loving and caring look. It soon achieved what other teachers had been unable to manage in over a year. For the first time the child said something of her own free will to the teacher, and for the first time she started to draw and to paint. But great faith and considerable patience are often needed before we can trust in powerless love and its transforming power. It often takes a very long time, for example, before a mother's love is rewarded by a positive reaction from a son whose behaviour has been vile and intolerable.

Our love seems even more powerless in the social and political field. What, for instance, can our love do against the overwhelming force of modern weapons? The examples of Sadat of Egypt, Gandhi in India, and Martin Luther King in the USA seem to be exceptions. In spite of all the endless talks, debates and discussions about the non-violent road to peace, recent events seem to show that peace cannot be secured without the backing of a certain degree of armed force. Yet weapons not only bring peace but constantly result in war. The non-violent, powerless love of many human beings is like the seed-corn that grows into a mighty tree in the shade of which people can live together in peace and concord. It is like the yeast that penetrates and works on a vastly greater amount of dough.

A monk I know said once that to transform a community of two hundred brothers you needed only three monks who were seriously prepared to work with complete devotion and love. Perhaps we need only thirty people who are open to God's love to start an entire nation moving in the right direction. If you really believe in the power of love, at least you will not feel totally powerless in the face of the present world situation. You can set your love over against it, even though years pass without the least evidence of any change. If you believe in the power of love to change things, your faith will enable you to counter the resignation and despair to which so many people succumb because they can do nothing about cruelty and warmongering.

Of course you cannot demonstrate the power of your love. You can only believe and hope that the seed of love will prosper and bear rich fruit.

Summary

Self-esteem and powerlessness are the two main determining factors of many people's lives today. They long to acquire a firm sense and conviction of their own worth and to trust in themselves. They want to live in a state of self-awareness, self-confidence, and self-assurance. They want to find out and then live explicitly as who they really are. They want to pierce through to their own uniqueness, to unravel the mystery of their own specific existence, and to reveal its secret truth. They want to discover and know their very own selves. They want to find out how to be well-defined, confident individuals when they are with other people.

The crowds of young people who attend our New Year, Easter, and Pentecost courses are seeking, on a basis of faith, not only a meaning for their lives but often a greater feeling of their own value. They hope that prayer will help them to find themselves, to sense their God-given dignity and worth, to overcome their fear and insecurity in a cold, anonymous world, and to discover real confidence. This means reaching a state of trust in God, and doing so in a community of people who accept and support one another. They must also trust in themselves, in the power that God has given them, and in the future that God holds in store for them.

Young people nowadays are scarcely—if at all—interested in questions of dogmatic theology; in what they ought to believe. As far as they are concerned, any remaining differences between Catholics and Protestants, for example, are almost totally unimportant today. As for philosophical questions of the kind that young people were passionately taken up by after the Second World War and into the 1970s, if they think of them at all they treat them as peripheral to their main interests and worries. The young people I see now are concerned above all to know how to live in this world meaningfully and confidently; how to see themselves in a new light; and how God can give them both an unshakeable conviction of their own worth and self-confidence.

Sometimes, to be sure, a relentless pursuit of self-valuation may betray an underlying narcissism. Some young people ignore the world situation. They can't bear— or just don't want—to think about Kosovo or Ruanda, or wherever the latest terrifying process of ethnic persecution or violence is taking place. So they turn to religious groups or sects for friendliness, security, and a refuge from this frighteningly, inexplicably hostile world. They are overwhelmed by their inability to do anything about the many wars and injustices in this world. They can't adjust to this powerlessness with regard to the big issues because they feel they haven't the power they need merely to withstand and overcome their own weaknesses and ineffectual selves. Because their sense of helplessness with respect to themselves and the world situation is so strong, they have to repress their awareness of a reality they can't do anything about.

The evidence of people's individual powerlessness everywhere in our world is unmistakable and overwhelming. You only have to look at the words and behaviour of politicians, economists, and ecclesiastics to realize how widespread it is. Trying to cope with our inability to influence and act on life is very distressing and unpleasant. So we try to ignore it and just walk away from it.

But, as the Bible tells us, powerlessness is an inescapable part of our lives. We can't pretend it isn't there. The people of Israel constantly experienced this same lack of power in the course of their history. Theirs was no history of growing power but one of increasing helplessness, until it culminated in exile and they had to begin all over again on a very small and modest scale.

As Christians, we look to Jesus Christ, who eventually experienced the helplessness of the cross. But God's power was revealed in Christ and, indeed, through the powerlessness of the cross. This divine strength is the power of resurrection that hauls us up and out of our helpless state. It is revealed to us in our very powerlessness as God's and not our own strength. The faith that confronts us with our powerlessness also shows us ways of using and dealing with it creatively, instead of seeking refuge in resignation or depression. This faith tells us how we can actively accept the demands that powerlessness makes on us, and how we can use prayer to shape our world in more human and Christlike ways.

The way of faith can help us to develop a sound feeling of our own dignity and value. It can show us how to tackle and work on our powerlessness so that it becomes a source of imagination and creativity.

But, if we do decide to follow the road of faith, we must remember that this also means taking very human paths in order to arrive at the truth and resolve our difficulties. Religion doesn't offer us a kind of short-cut, or spiritual bypass. Convictions of value and feelings of powerlessness alike have their origins in psychological reality. They originate in what has actually happened to people: in childhood experiences and in the felt events of everyday life. Consequently faith has to take psychological knowledge, awareness, and understanding seriously before it can help us to define a way out of our problems that extends beyond that psychological level.

We would not really be helping people whom a difficult childhood had prevented from developing a sense of personal worth, if we assured them prematurely that all they had to do to be confident and self-assured was simply to acknowledge that God trusted in them. That is not enough. Believers also have to confront the facts of their own psychological history and mental attitudes. They have to face the psychic wounds or traumas of their childhood in prayer before God, and to examine them together with their pastors, priests, therapists, or counsellors. Their psychic injuries will never heal until they reach down to the whole truth about themselves and uncover it before God and another human being. Then, in spite of all their traumas and illnesses, they will discover their own divine worth and begin to develop a real sense of their own value. In faith and trust they will see and hear the implications of God's fundamental message for his Son Jesus when he was baptized in the river Jordan.

God is saying the same absolutely vital thing to us now. He makes exactly the same promise as we stand in the water of our particular Jordan, even if we are up to our necks in guilt and failure: "You are my Son, you are my Daughter, my Beloved, on you my favour rests" (Mark 1:11). If we listen to that message and learn from it, as we emerge from the water we may find that heaven is beginning to open for us, and that the Spirit is descending on us too.

Notes

1. Cf Erik H. Erikson, *Identity and the Life-cycle* (London & New York, 1968).
2. *Ibid.*
3. John Bradshaw, *Homecoming: Reclaiming and Championing your Inner Child* (New York, 1990; London 1991).
4. Virginia Satir, *Peoplemaking* (New York, 1972).
5. C. J. Jung, *Collected Works*, Vol. 16: *The Practice of Psychotherapy*, trans. R. F. C. Hull (2d ed., London & New York, 1966), p. 59.
6. C. G. Jung, *Collected Works*, Vol. 10: *Civilization in Transition*, trans. R. F. C. Hull (London & New York, 1964), p. 271.
7. C. G. Jung, *Briefe*, Vol. 1 (Olten, 1972), pp. 198ff.
8. Roberto Assagioli, *Psychosynthese. Prinzipien, Methoden und Techniken* (Zurich, 1988), p. 139.
9. James F. G. Bugental, *Intimate Journeys* (San Francisco, 1990)
10. Alfred Adler, *What Life Should Mean to You* (London & New York, 1932).
11. Karl Frielingsdorf, *Vom Überleben zum Leben [From Survival to Life]* (Mainz, 1989).
12. Evagrius Ponticus, *Brief aus der Wüste [Letters from the Wilderness;* tr. from the Greek] (Trier, 1986), p. 39.
13. Franz Müller "Ohnmacht" [Powerlessness], in *Praktisches Lexikon der Spiritualität*, ed. Christian Schütz (Freiburg im Breisgau, 1988), pp. 942ff.
14. Heinz Henseler, "Die Theorie des Narzissismus" [The Theory of Narcissism], in *Psychologie des 20. Jahrhunderts*, Vol. 2, ed. Dieter Eickem (Zurich, 1976), p. 463.
15. *Ibid.*, p. 464.
16. *Ibid.*, p. 465.
17. John Bradshaw, *op. cit.*
18. Franz Furger, "Macht" [Power], in *Praktisches Lexikon der Spiritualität, op. cit.*, p. 823.
19. Karl Rahner, "Theology of Power," in *Theological Investigations* IV (London & New York, 1966), p. 391.

20. Klaus Hemmerle, "Power," in *Sacramentum Mundi*, Vol. 5, eds K. Rahner, C. Ernst, and K. Smyth (London & New York, 1970), p. 72.
21. Martin Buber, *Tales of the Hasidim*, Vol. 2 (New York & London, 1961), p. 201.
22. Dietrich Bonhoeffer, *Letters and Papers from Prison* (London, 1953); *Prisoner for God* (New York, 1953), p. 122 (cf also pp. 122-32).
23. Staretz Siluan [Monk of Mount Athos], *Leben, Lehre, Schriften*, ed. Archimandrite Sophronius (Düsseldorf, 1959), p. 146.

The Author

Anselm Gruen is a monk of the Benedictine Abbey of Münsterschwarzach near Würzburg in southern Germany. He is an extremely popular religious writer with a number of best-selling books on the market in a number of  languages. His highly original yet practical approach to theology combines his profound knowledge of both religion and psychology with special reference to C. G. Jung, the founder of Analytical Psychology. Fr Gruen writes books in order to help people by encouraging them really to "live their lives." This means looking for God in themselves, making something of themselves, and changing the way they are and behave. This approach is evident in his first book published in English, *Angels of Grace* (1998).

Anselm Gruen was born in Junkerhausen in the Rhön area of Germany, where his family, originally from Munich, was evacuated during the Second World War. He grew up in Munich. In 1964 he took his school-leaving examination at the boarding school where he was educated and in the same year decided to become a Benedictine monk.

He studied theology from 1965 to 1971 at Saint Ottilien and in Rome. He wrote his doctoral thesis on Karl Rahner's theology and concept of salvation. He obtained his final qualification as a teacher at university and further education level in 1974. He then studied economics and financial management until 1976. The following year he was appointed adminstrator of the abbey of

Münsterschwarzach, where he also directs residential courses in meditation techniques, psychoanalytical interpretation of dreams, fasting, and contemplation.

The abbey was founded in 815 and closed in 1803 but re-opened in 1913. It runs twenty flourishing trades and businesses, including a publishing house, a printshop, a goldsmith's, and a bookshop, all of which contribute to the monastery's finances. As a result, the abbey is largely self-supporting, and voluntary contributions are devoted to missionary work.